The Glory
of Living
and
Study Guide

Dr. Myles Munroe

Destiny Image® Publishers, Inc.
P.O. Box 310
Shippensburg, PA 17257-0310

"Speaking to the Purposes of God for This
Generation and for the Generations to Come"

Diplomat Press, The Diplomat Center
Carmichael Road, P. O. Box N-9583
Nassau, Bahamas

ISBN 0-7684-2298-1

(Formerly published as *The Purpose and Power of God's Glory* ISBN 0-7684-2119-5
and as *The Purpose and Power of God's Glory Study Guide* ISBN 0-7684-2149-7)

For Worldwide Distribution
Printed in the U.S.A.

This book and all other Destiny Image, Revival Press, MercyPlace, Fresh Bread, Destiny Image Fiction, and Treasure House books are available at Christian bookstores and distributors worldwide.

2 3 4 5 6 7 8 9 10 / 09 08 07 06 05

For a U.S. bookstore nearest you, call **1-800-722-6774**.
For more information on foreign distributors, call **717-532-3040**.
Or reach us on the Internet: **www.destinyimage.com**

The Glory of Living

Dedication

To my beloved daughter, Charisa, a gift to me from the heavenly Father who is full of glory and grace. Your name means "gift of God," and it is my hope that you will manifest your full glory in your lifetime and bless the world with your true nature. Your spirit of adventure and confidence is an inspiration to me and I have no doubt you will impact the world beyond your dreams. This book was inspired by your passion for life.

To my beloved son, "Chairo" Myles Junior, whose quiet spirit and disciplined life has made me a proud father and inspired this book. The world has yet to see your true potential and the hidden glory of your life. I am certain that you will make your mark in history and change your world for the better. Remember, always believe the dream in your heart and never doubt your ability to achieve your goals. May your full glory be manifested in your generation and beyond.

To the millions of people in the developing and third world countries—I am committed to helping you discover, develop, and release the glory that has been hidden many years by the darkness of historical oppression, suppression, and intimidation. May the undiscovered glory of a people be manifested in your generation.

Endorsements

Myles Munroe has the unique ability to search out and bring forth the practical meaning out of spiritual truth, to carefully remove the exterior coverings of religious jargon and spiritual cliches that obscure spiritual reality. He has done it again with *The Glory of Living.* Thousands have preached on the glory but few have exposed us to the spiritual depths of the glory of the Lord as Myles has done. Myles will open your eyes to the reflected glory of God inside you as you have never seen it before.

This is not a "touchy, feel-good" kind of book. It takes the mystery out of the glory, unveiling powerful truths that unlock new vistas of His glorious presence, while portraying practical steps to walking in that glory.

Don Nori
Publisher, Destiny Image, Inc.

Dr. Myles Munroe's newest book, *The Glory of Living,* is a breath of fresh air for discouraged and disheartened people, believers and non-believers alike, who feel trapped in a mundane and mediocre existence. His insight on the hidden glory residing in each of us is the perfect prescription to inject new life and hope into weary hearts, infuse fresh excitement and meaning into ordinary lives, and lift readers into higher realms of realized potential and fulfillment of God's purposes in the earth.

Dr. Paul F. Crouch
President, Trinity Broadcast Network

You have a treasure hidden deep within you—a tangible "glory" to manifest God's divine purpose for your life. In *The Glory of Living*, Dr. Myles Munroe demonstrates how to release the true essence of your heavenly calling in order to fully glorify the Lord. As you read this book, allow His spirit to change you supernaturally from glory to glory!

Rod Parsley
Pastor, World Harvest Church, Columbus, Ohio
Host, *Breakthrough* Television Broadcast

Contents

	Preface	11
	Introduction	13
Chapter One	The Nature of Glory	17
Chapter Two	The Environment of Glory	29
Chapter Three	Glory in an "Earth Suit"	49
Chapter Four	The Glory of "Becoming"	65
Chapter Five	The Presence and the Glory	85
Chapter Six	Restoring the Environment of Glory	99
Chapter Seven	Squeezing the Glory Out	113
Chapter Eight	Jesus—Revealing God's Glory	131
Chapter Nine	Releasing the Glory	147
Chapter Ten	The Fragrance of Glory	161

The Glory of Living Study Guide 177

Preface

Glory is the goal of life. There is no greater purpose in life than to expose your personal glory. It is a fact of creation that every living thing possesses its own glory and exists for the purpose of manifesting that glory.

If the greatest tragedy in life is not death but life without a purpose, then the greatest shame in life is not revealing your true glory. The cemeteries of earth are filled with the glory of many who failed to access their true selves, and left the earth without ever showing their real worth. The question is: Why do so many individuals live an entire life never experiencing the glory of their lives, while others live to taste the glory of a full and fulfilled life?

A few days ago I stood on the beautiful sandy beaches of the Bahamas and watched the graceful flight of the sea gulls on the current of the sea breezes. *What elegance*! I thought. Turning to my wife I said, "Look at that bird in its glory." Suddenly I realized I had just summed up all of life. Like that bird, we must all strive to "be in our glory." Have you ever observed a giant cedar tree, and the majestic beauty of a royal oak tree? At full strength we say they are in their glory. The seeds of these great trees hid their glory and concealed their full weight. The same is true of the musician who writes and produces music. The work is his glory.

I believe that this issue of glory is the most important aspect of creation and that it holds the key to fulfillment and personal satisfaction. The word *glory* in its fundamental meaning connotes such concepts as "full weight," "true nature," "full essence" or "true reality." Therefore, the glory of a thing is its true essence and nature. The Creator designed all things with their glory, or true essence, buried within. Therefore glory is the hidden truth of all created things. The purpose of life is to manifest that glory.

You and every one of the people on this planet are walking containers of glory, and it is the Creator's desire that each one release that full glory and fill the earth with the glory of their Manufacturer. Yet the question is: How do you accomplish this? I wrote this book to provide you with keys and principles to assist you. It is my hope and desire that you will truly tap into your hidden glory and fill your generation with the fragrance of your life. May the following pages stir in your spirit the inspiration, motivation, and passion to complete your God-given purpose, and to move daily from glory to glory to glory.

Introduction

He was a stately figure in the winner's circle, his bulging muscles shining in the midday sun with the sweat of a hard run race. The crowd cheered as the wreath of beautiful roses was placed around his powerful neck. His rider sat up straight to pose for the camera and to receive the coveted trophy at the envy of the losers. It was a proud moment. After many years of careful development, grooming, training, and practice, the stallion stood there in his full glory.

The scene has been repeated thousands of times in life. The moment when creation stands in its full bloom, be it a flower, a bird, a butterfly or a great white shark, we experience their moment of glory. This glory exists in everything and everyone. Every animal, plant, star, and human being possesses glory consistent with their purpose for being. Even the Creator Himself is said to be full of glory.

Each year thousands travel to the ancient city of Rome to visit historical sites frozen in time. One of the most sought-out sites is the Sistine Chapel. Tourists come by the busloads to look at and photograph the work of the great master Michelangelo. The masterpiece painted on the ceiling of this revered chapel has become one of the great wonders of the world and serves as a standard for developing artists. What is this work that generates so much attention and pride? It is simply the glory of a man. It is the manifestation of the hidden glory of the artist. In other words, Michelangelo filled the earth with his glory and left the essence of his life and nature in the earth.

Many people walk around with their masterpiece in their minds, buried under wishful thinking, procrastination, fear, excuses, and intimidation. What a tragedy! Suppose Michelangelo had died with these works of art in his mind. What a waste that would have been! He worshiped with his work, manifesting his glory in his generation and ours.

As I look at the creation around me I see glory everywhere. The seed exposes its glory as a tree, the caterpillar as a butterfly, the eaglet as an eagle, the boy as a man, and the girl as a woman. I am reminded of the great basketball player, Michael Jordan, whose high school coach said that he would never play basketball as a pro. Yet Michael believed the dream he carried and worked at developing and perfecting his game. Today he stands as an athletic icon for millions. To see him on the court is to see him in his true glory. His gift from God is his athletic ability. Others may have the hidden glory of music, art, writing, baking, acting, designing, or managing. Whatever your gift and talent, that is your glory and it was given to fill the earth.

God the Creator is a God of glory who created everything to expose His glory. Glory is the full manifestation of your purpose, which is your true self. However, just as a fish needs water, and a seed needs soil to bring forth its full glory, even so you and I need the right environment to manifest our true nature. Glory is released when the conditions are right and demands are made on it. Glory is the true essence of a thing and is self-manifestation. As the destruction of a seed is the death of a tree, so the suppression or retardation of human potential is the destruction of glory.

Every invention is the manifestation of someone's glory. The telephone is the glory of Alexander Graham Bell. The television, the toaster, the video machine, the car, the computer—all are the manifestation of someone's glory. I wonder what great invention, work of art, ministry, product, or business lies as untapped glory within you? I challenge you to not take your glory to the cemetery, but rather to manifest it before you die.

This book itself is a part of my manifested glory; there are many more waiting to be released. It is my desire to release all of my glory and share it around the world. It is my hope that you also will dedicate yourself to glorifying the Creator by working out your glory for His honor.

For many people the word *glory* is not a practical concept, but rather a nebulous metaphysical idea reserved for the intangible. In the religious domain it has been ascribed in worship only to God— as His inherent attribute alone.

But the concept of *glory* is practical and relevant not only to God but to all of His creation. David the great king of Israel declared, "The heavens declare the glory of God; the skies proclaim the work of His hands" (Ps. 19:1).

Glory is the manifestation of one's nature through one's work. In essence, when we use our gifts and talents to realize visions and dreams given by the Creator, we are manifesting our glory.

You are created to glorify your Creator through the productivity of your works. Therefore, glorifying God is not limited to praising Him, but rather to putting your hand to productive, wholesome, and positive work. It is interesting that one of the foundational meanings of the word *worship* is "to work." It is time for us to realize that all men possess glory and have this hidden treasure of their Creator crying out for exposure. It is my belief that the Creator desires all men everywhere, male and female, to manifest their glory. Only He has the ultimate prescription for its full release. I dare *you* to move to the next level of your life and decide to go from

❖ The Glory of Living

glory to glory. You owe it to yourself and your Creator. Let men see your good works and glorify your Father who is in Heaven (see Matt. 5:16).

Chapter One

The Nature of Glory

All of Creation exists
to manifest the glory of God.

Everywhere we turn, we are surrounded by glory. If we but have eyes to see it, glory is all around us. There is glory in every tree, in every flower, and in every blade of grass. Every living creature displays glory: every bird, every fish, every insect and creeping thing, as well as every mammal, from the great elephant in the jungle to the tiny mouse in the field. Glory shines forth from the sun, the moon, the stars, and all the other heavenly bodies sprinkled across the vast canopy of space. There is glory in every human being on earth; you have it and so do I. Glory resides in every created thing. The glory we see in Creation, however, is but the barest reflection of the greater glory of the Creator.

King David the psalmist wrote,

The heavens declare the glory of God; the skies proclaim the work of His hands (Psalms 19:1).

❖ The Glory of Living

In Isaiah's vision of Heaven the seraphim called out to one another,

Holy, holy, holy is the Lord Almighty; the whole earth is full of His glory (Isaiah 6:3b).

The apostle Paul referred to the glory in all things when he wrote to the Corinthians,

There are also celestial bodies, and bodies terrestrial: but the glory of the celestial is one, and the glory of the terrestrial is another. There is one glory of the sun, and another glory of the moon, and another glory of the stars: for one star differeth from another star in glory (1 Corinthians 15:40-41 KJV).

Glory Is the Full Expression of God's Nature

What is glory? What do we mean when we speak of the "glory of God" or the "glory" of the sun, moon, and stars? The Hebrew word for "glory," as found in Psalm 19:1 and Isaiah 6:3 (and nearly 200 other places in the Old Testament) is *kabod,* which comes from a root word with the basic meaning of "heavy," or "weighty." *Kabod* also carries the idea of "fullness" or the "full weight" of something. In this sense it refers to the "weightiness" of someone of high importance, a person of notable, impressive, and positive reputation. When used in the phrase, "the glory of God," *kabod* most often refers to "a visible manifestation of God" that is "directly related to God's self-disclosure and His intent to dwell among men."[1]

In Scripture verses such as Isaiah 6:3 and others that speak of God's glory filling the earth, *kabod* refers to "that reputation for greatness which God alone deserves, not only because of His natural position as king, but because of His unsurpassed activity as

---

1. R. Laird Harris et al., ed., *Theological Wordbook of the Old Testament,* Vol. 1 (Chicago, IL: Moody Press, 1980), p. 427.

❖ 18

deliverer and savior…It is not merely God's reputation which fills the earth, but it is the very reality of His presence."[2] The greatest and ultimate display of God's glory on earth was in the person of His Son, Jesus Christ, of whom the apostle John wrote, "We have seen His glory, the glory of the One and Only, who came from the Father, full of grace and truth" (Jn. 1:14b). "Through [Jesus] and through His presence in the church, God's glory is indeed filling the earth."[3]

In the New Testament, the basic Greek word for "glory," as in First Corinthians 15:40-41 and John 1:14, is *doxa*, from which we get our word *doxology*. Essentially, *doxa* refers to the attributes or true nature of a thing. It is used to describe "the nature and acts of God in self-manifestation, i.e., what He essentially is and does, as exhibited in whatever way He reveals Himself in these respects, and particularly in the person of Christ."[4] *Doxa* is "the manifested perfection of [God's] character, especially His righteousness," and "the exhibition of His attributes and ways."[5] The "glory" (*doxa*) of God refers to the characteristic qualities of His nature, which are best seen through the person of Jesus Christ and the lives of believers.

So when we speak of the "glory" (*kabod* or *doxa*) of God, we are referring to the weightiness of His person and reputation, the fullness of His presence in the earth, the visible manifestation of His attributes and character, and the full expression of His nature. Wow!

---

2.   Harris, *Theological Wordbook of the Old Testament*.

3.   Harris, *Theological Wordbook of the Old Testament*.

4.   W. E. Vine et al., *Vine's Complete Expository Dictionary of Old and New Testament Words* (Nashville, TN: Thomas Nelson Publishers, 1985), New Testament section, p. 267.

5.   Vine, *Vine's Dictionary of Old and New Testament Words*, New Testament section, pp. 267-268.

Glory Is God Putting Himself on Display

To put it another way, **the glory of God is the full nature of God on display.** That's why Psalm 19:1 says, "The heavens declare the glory of God." The Hebrew word for "declare" also means to "show forth," and another word for "show forth" is "display." Whenever we gaze at the splendor of the night sky above us or soak up the beauty of the natural world around us we see the creative quality of God on display. **God is a Creator by nature, and His creation displays His creativity.** Creation manifests God's glory. The splendor of creation points us to God, and we attribute that characteristic quality to His nature.

> **The glory of God is the full nature of God on display.**

Again, from the pen of David we have

Ascribe to the Lord, O mighty ones, ascribe to the Lord glory and strength. Ascribe to the Lord the glory due His name; worship the Lord in the splendor of His holiness (Psalm 29:1-2).

To "ascribe" something means to "attribute" to someone a specific action, behavior, or quality of character. Whenever we recognize a particular trait as being characteristic of someone, we consider that trait to be an "attribute" of that person's character or nature. Looking closely at the word *attribute*, we see that it means to give "a tribute" to someone; to offer respect, gratitude, love, or appreciation and to acknowledge that person's worth, honor, integrity, service, and accomplishment.

In a way, when we attribute something to someone, we are "blaming" that person for that action, but in a positive sense. When we attribute Creation to God, we are "blaming" Him for it. God is the "guilty" party. He alone is responsible for Creation. In creation, we see the glory of the Creator. God has put Himself on display.

The Four Principles of Glory in Creation

There are several principles we can note about the relationship between glory and creation. The first principle is, *God created everything with glory*. The opening verse of the Bible is a simple statement about God's basic nature: "In the beginning God created the heavens and the earth" (Gen. 1:1). Because God is a Creator by nature, it is only natural that His creation would reflect His glory.

As I have already said, glory resides in every created thing, whether on earth or in the heavens. Everything God made has its own unique glory, which reflects His glory. Birds, cats, dogs, ants, mosquitoes, trees, flowers, sun, moon, stars—each have their own unique glory. That glory is the nature of God residing in every created thing, the hidden reality that God placed in each one and which holds the full essence and potential of what that creature is supposed to be and do.

This brings us to the second principle: *God created everything to manifest its glory*. God's original design was that every creature, by becoming everything it was created to be, would manifest its own unique glory and by so doing reveal God's glory. The words of the first chapter of Genesis make this clear.

> **Then God said, "Let the land produce vegetation: seed-bearing plants and trees on the land that bear fruit with seed in it, according to their various kinds." And it was so** (Genesis 1:11).

> **And God said, "Let there be lights in the expanse of the sky to separate the day from the night, and let them serve as signs to mark seasons and days and years, and let them be lights in the expanse of the sky to give light on the earth." And it was so** (Genesis 1:14-15).

> **And God said, "Let the water teem with living creatures, and let birds fly above the earth across the expanse of the sky"** (Genesis 1:20).

❖ The Glory of Living

> **And God said, "Let the land produce living creatures according to their kinds: livestock, creatures that move along the ground, and wild animals, each according to its kind." And it was so** (Genesis 1:24).

All of these things—plants, animals, birds, fish, heavenly bodies—were created to act or behave according to the nature God put into them. They were created to manifest their glory, "and it was so." It is a bird's glory to fly; God created it with "flight" nature. God doesn't add swim to a fish; it comes with "swim" nature. God doesn't put "moo" in the cow; the cow comes with "moo." That's the way God creates. The full nature of a creature—its glory—is already present when it is created. All it takes is nourishment, growth, and the right environment for that creature to fully display its glory.

> **The glory of man is to be like God and to rule like God in fellowship and harmony with God.**

The third principle is that *God is pleased when glory is seen.* Throughout the first chapter of Genesis we find God looking on His creation with pleasure, and expressing this pleasure in the words, "and saw that it was good." After creating light, "God saw that the light was good…" (Gen. 1:4). Each successive phase of creation—land and sea, vegetation, heavenly bodies, sea creatures and birds, and land animals—is followed by the statement, "And God saw that it was good" (Gen. 1:10b,12b,18b,21b,25b). Finally, after completing creation with His crowning achievement—man—"God saw all that He had made, and it was very good" (Gen. 1:31a). God is pleased when His creations manifest their glory—and His—by becoming everything He created them to be.

Finally, *God created man as the ultimate exposure of His glory.* God's purpose in creating the human race was so that we could live in fellowship with Him, rule over the earth as He rules in Heaven, and manifest His glory by fully displaying our own. If the lower ranks of creatures were designed to display God's glory, how much more were we, who represent the highest order of creation and the greatest masterpiece of God's artistry. If we think of God as an artist, then man is His masterpiece.

The Master's Masterpiece

After spending six days speaking worlds into existence and bringing forth the lower forms of life in all their infinite variety, God prepared for the climax of His grand and divine design.

> **Then God said, "Let Us make man in Our image, in Our likeness, and let them rule over the fish of the sea and the birds of the air, over the livestock, over all the earth, and over all the creatures that move along the ground." So God created man in His own image, in the image of God He created him; male and female He created them. God blessed them and said to them, "Be fruitful and increase in number; fill the earth and subdue it. Rule over the fish of the sea and the birds of the air and over every living creature that moves on the ground"** (Genesis 1:26-28).

All Creation displays God's glory, but only man was made in God's image.

When God set out to create man, He purposed to fashion a creature that was unique, unlike anything else He had made. These verses reveal two characteristics of man that set him apart from the rest of God's created order. First, man was created in the image of God Himself and, second, he was created to have dominion over the earth and all other life on it.

God said, "Let Us make man in Our image, in Our likeness." The Hebrew word *tselem* (image) also means "likeness," "resemblance," or "representation." It is the same word used elsewhere in the Old Testament for "idol." Since God is spirit and man is flesh, our likeness to Him is not in physical resemblance. Rather, God has endowed us with spiritual, intellectual, and moral likeness to Himself. Being created in the image of God means that He gave us His moral and spiritual nature. In other words, God created us to be like Him in nature, character, and attributes.

We were made to be like God in another way as well. God said, "Let them rule over the fish of the sea and the birds of the air, over the livestock, over all the earth, and over all the creatures that move along the ground." Just as God is sovereign and rules over all His creation, He created us to have dominion over the earth, ruling it as His co-regents. By God's design, we were created for rulership. That also is what it means to be made in the image of God.

Once He had finished forming the earth with all its natural resources and all its sea, plant, bird, and animal life, God said, "Now it's time to produce the manager of this planet." So He created man. The Hebrew word *adam* can refer either to an individual man or to all of mankind. In Genesis 1:26-27 it is used in the plural sense; God created all of humankind to hold dominion over the earth. He built into us the attributes, the character, and the drive to subdue and rule the natural order. If the glory of a bird is to fly and the glory of a fish is to swim, then the glory of man is to *be* like God and to *rule* like God in fellowship and harmony *with* God.

Man Alone Was Created in the Image of God

It is this built-in, God-given capacity for rulership that causes people in any culture to chafe under slavery or oppression. We were not created to be slaves, but to rule over the created order. Notice that the dominion of man includes the earth and all plant and animal life on it. Ruling over other human beings, particularly in an oppressive manner, is *not* within the original God-given jurisdiction of any person. Human government of laws was a necessary consequence of man's fall, instituted by God to protect the innocent and the helpless and to restrict the spread of sin.

God created us uniquely in His own image, possessing His nature and glory and attributes. Since all humans were created to rule the earth under God's overall sovereignty, it would be a contradiction for Him then to decree that any of us should be relegated to a life of subservience to anyone else. God is the King of creation, the Lord of the universe, and the owner of all things. He is the Power of all powers, almighty, awesome, invincible, and untouchable. God is God, and He took a little part of Himself and poured it out into us.

That means that whatever our Daddy got, we got. Everything God ever intended us to be we already have—virtually infinite potential hidden inside these earthly bodies. God created us to have dominion over the earth; anything less squanders our potential.

All creation displays God's glory, but only man was made in God's image. Birds display God's glory but they were not created in His image. Plants display God's glory, but they were not created in His image. The earth displays God's glory, but it was not created in His image. Of all the created order, man alone possesses the spirit and capacity to subdue the earth and rule over it. **In man alone resides the image of God, the unique stamp of our Creator that sets us apart from every other creature.**

In the art world art critics and experts are always on the lookout for imitations. To the amateur and untrained eye, a fake can easily be mistaken for a genuine masterpiece. Art forgers are that skillful. An expert, however, can readily identify a genuine original. For someone who knows what to look for, the telltale characteristics of any particular master are unmistakable in his or her work.

In financial institutions, tellers and others who regularly handle large amounts of money are trained to recognize counterfeit currency. They learn this skill not by studying examples of counterfeit bills but by studying the genuine article. Once they have thoroughly learned what the real thing looks like, they can easily identify a fake when they see it.

❖ The Glory of Living

Human beings are God's representatives on earth. He created us in His image. We are not fake imitations. We are genuine masterpieces "painted" by the hand of the Master Artist. We are not counterfeits but the genuine article. No other creature in all creation has that distinction. Sin has distorted God's image and hidden it away under a lot of worldly "junk," so we are hard to identify as "God's originals." He has the power to dig down and cut through the junk to expose the glory—the telltale characteristics of His hand—that hides in each of us. He wants to display us as the masterpieces we are. That's why His glory is so important.

Nothing Is More Important Than the Glory of God

After all my years of Bible study, seminary training, preaching, and teaching, and after all the books I have read, I have come to the conclusion and conviction *that nothing is more important than the glory of God.* Everything in creation—plants, animals, birds, fish, the oceans, the mountains, the multiplied millions of stars within our own galaxy, the millions of galaxies scattered throughout the infinite expanse of space—was designed with God's glory in mind. God is a Creator, and creativity cries out for expression. So, God created a vast universe through which to express Himself. All of creation exists to express, to reveal, to display, and to manifest the glory of God.

If the most important thing to God is His glory, it is also the most important thing to us, who were created to live with Him and rule under Him as stewards of the earth. *We were created to expose God's glory,* but in a way different from the rest of creation. God's original and unchanging desire was for man to expose His glory in a way that no other creature could. That's why He created us in His image. God designed human beings to be the ultimate expression in creation of who He is and what He is like. We are unique. Not even the angels in Heaven were created in God's image.

We can fulfill our purpose as carriers and exposers of God's glory only as long as we live in the right environment and maintain the right relationship with Him. The "religious" answer to the question "Why did God create us?" is "to worship Him." Our true purpose is to display God's glory. That, however, is what true worship is all about.

Worship is not something we "go to" on Sunday, or Saturday, or Friday, or whenever. Worship is a *state* that we should remain in all the time. Perfect worship is living continually in the *presence* of God (the proper environment) and enjoying continual *fellowship* with God (the proper relationship). God created us for intimacy with Him. That's what worship is: an ongoing intimate relationship with God.

From the very beginning, God provided both the proper environment and the proper relationship in which the humans He had created could thrive and fully express their glory as beings living and working in harmony with Him. At the same time, they would manifest the glory of God by becoming everything He created them to be.

Sin marred both the environment and the relationship. Man failed to realize his glory and thus distorted the image of God in which he was made. God's glory was so important to Him that He would do whatever was necessary to protect it. God's love for His highest creation was so great that He would do whatever was necessary to restore sinful man to his original position of intimate relationship in the environment of his Creator's presence.

❖   PRINCIPLES   ❖

1. Glory resides in every created thing.

2. The glory of God is the full nature of God on display.

3. God created everything with glory.

4. God created everything to manifest its glory.

5. God is pleased when glory is seen.

6. God created us to expose His glory.

7. The glory of man is to be like God and to rule like God in fellowship and harmony with God.

8. All creation displays God's glory, but only man was made in God's image.

9. Nothing is more important than God's glory.

10. Perfect worship is living continually in the presence of God and enjoying continual fellowship with God.

Chapter Two

The Environment of Glory

The presence of God is
the perfect environment for our fruitfulness.

Every living thing needs a proper environment in which to display its God-given glory. A bird was created to fly; therefore, the glory of a bird is to fly. Birds need the sky and the open air to fully express their glory. If you take a bird and lock it in a cage, it cannot show its full glory. The bird's glory is restricted by its environment.

A fish was created to swim; therefore, the glory of a fish is to swim. Only in water can it give its glory full expression. It is natural for a fish to swim. That which is natural to a thing is its glory. A fish doesn't struggle in the water; it swims. Swimming is its glory. When I see fish swim, I get jealous. They don't have to wear snorkels, or air tanks, or masks and fins; they simply…swim. That's their nature. When I go in the water, I struggle just to keep up. The fish all crowd around me and laugh.

❖ The Glory of Living

On the other hand, if I take a fish out of its watery environment, it will start having problems immediately. It will flop around for dear life and begin to suffocate. If I do not put it back into the water, it will die within minutes. A fish can't breathe in a dry environment. Its gills are designed to filter oxygen from water. Only in the water can a fish survive and thrive. Only in its proper environment can a fish display its glory.

The environment we live in is deadly for a fish, and the fish's environment is deadly for us unless we carry part of our environment along in the form of air tanks and masks. Likewise, we cannot enter a bird's domain without the assistance of some kind of artificial flying machine, such as an airplane, helicopter, hang glider or hot-air balloon.

Like the bird and the fish, mankind was also created to function in a prescribed environment: the presence of God. We thrive best in the environment for which we were designed. Our glory is to be like God and to rule like God in fellowship and harmony with God. Like a bird in a cage, anything that hinders us from becoming everything God created us to be restricts our glory. The only way we can really learn how to be like God and to rule like God is to live in an environment that is permeated with the presence of God. In order to be like God, we must know God, and to know God, we must spend time in His presence.

Before God created life on the earth, He prepared suitable environments according to what every variety and species would need. He established the oceans, lakes, and rivers in their proper places, then filled them with aquatic life. He set apart the dry land with a temperate climate and all the soil nutrients necessary for plant life to flourish. That plant life then provided nourishment for the land animals and birds that followed.

Man, God's greatest creation, needed something more. A moderate climate and plenty of fruits, herbs, and vegetables to eat were not enough for beings made in God's own image. In order for them to function properly and fully display their glory, Adam and Eve needed an environment where they were surrounded by the presence of God, a place where they could be in continual union with Him. God provided just such a place. The Bible calls it Eden.

Man's Ideal Environment

Before God created man, He prepared an environment perfectly suited to him.

> **The Lord God formed the man from the dust of the ground and breathed into his nostrils the breath of life, and the man became a living being. Now the Lord God had planted a garden in the east, in Eden; and there He put the man He had formed. And the Lord God made all kinds of trees grow out of the ground—trees that were pleasing to the eye and good for food. In the middle of the garden were the tree of life and the tree of the knowledge of good and evil....The Lord God took the man and put him in the Garden of Eden to work it and take care of it. And the Lord God commanded the man, "You are free to eat from any tree in the garden; but you must not eat from the tree of the knowledge of good and evil, for when you eat of it you will surely die"** (Genesis 2:7-9;15-17).

The Scripture says that "the Lord God *had planted* a garden in the east, in Eden." The use of the past perfect tense here suggests that God fashioned the garden before He formed the man who was to tend it. Judging from the description, the Garden of Eden must have been a beautiful and pleasant place. This is only to be expected since God intended it as a home for His greatest creation.

The word *Eden* is a direct transliteration from the Hebrew. Although its origin is uncertain, it probably stems from the primitive root *adan*, which means "soft," or "pleasant" (Strong's, H5727). As it appears in Genesis 2:8 and 15, *eden* means "pleasure," or "delight" (Strong's H5730, H5731). The Garden of Eden, therefore, could also be called the Garden of Delight. In other parts of the Old Testament, particularly in Isaiah and Ezekiel, *eden* is referred to as the "garden of God," or the "garden of the Lord."

All of these meanings put together show that there was more to the Garden of Eden than simply a geographical location. It represented a state of pure, complete, and unbroken fellowship between God and man. Eden was a special spot on the earth that God chose, where the unseen world touched the seen world, where the spiritual met the physical. It was an open door between Heaven and earth, a place where the presence of God covered like a cloud. The Garden of Eden was a unique spot on the earth in which lay an open door to God's presence. Eden was more an environment than a location.

First, God made man (Heb. *adam*) in His own image, then He placed man in His presence to live, to work, and to thrive. Eden was the perfect environment for Adam to bring forth all he was and thereby display his glory. By functioning fully just as he was created, Adam would bring glory to God. As long as he remained in the Garden, Adam experienced perfect joy and complete fulfillment in the presence of his Creator.

> **E**den represented a state of pure, complete, and unbroken fellowship between God and man.

Adam found not only the presence of God in the Garden; he also found purpose. Human beings cannot experience complete fulfillment in life unless they find purpose in life. Fulfillment comes with purpose. God gave Adam purposeful work to do in the Garden. Adam didn't spend his time lying around lazily popping grapes into his mouth. He had the responsibility to "work" the garden and "take care of it." By God's design, Adam was steward of the Garden and master of the created order. That was his "glory." The glory of man was to expose and manifest God's nature and character through his exercise of dominion in the earth by his inherent gifts, talents, and abilities.

Filling the Earth With God's Glory

God's original purpose extended beyond the Garden. He wanted Eden to be duplicated throughout the world so that His glory truly would fill the earth. This, too, was to be part of man's glory. Within the environment of the Garden, God made Eve to be Adam's mate, partner, and companion. Then He told them, "Be fruitful and increase in number; fill the earth and subdue it" (Gen. 1:28b). Being fruitful means to bring out that which is on the inside; to expose the hidden glory. To be fruitful means to be productive, as well as to reproduce oneself.

What is the true glory of an apple tree? To produce apples. Everything needed for the production of apples is already in the tree, but until the ripe, red fruit appears on the branches, the tree has not fully displayed its glory. It has not completely fulfilled God's purpose. In Matthew 21:19 Jesus cursed an unfruitful fig tree. In Luke 13:6-9 He tells a parable about a vineyard owner who wanted his servant to cut down a fig tree that had produced no fruit in three years. Fruitfulness is important to God. It is part of His creative design and fundamental to His nature.

God instructed Adam and Eve to "increase in number" and "fill the earth." The King James Version of Genesis 1:28 says, "multiply, and replenish the earth." All of these words involve the principles of reproduction and duplication. God wanted them not only to reproduce themselves by having children, but also to reproduce their environment. He said, in effect, "Adam, begin here in this Garden. I want you and Eve to have children—lots of children. I want you to raise a righteous seed who will grow up loving My presence the way you do. I want you, through them, to duplicate this paradise, this 'Eden' of My presence, over and over and over until the whole earth is filled with My glory."

It was a grand design befitting the mind of an infinite, omnipotent Creator. Adam and Eve were fashioned to function in fellowship with God. His presence was the only environment they needed. Under His covering they were completely free to be fruit-ful, to multiply, and to become everything He intended for them to be. Only in God's presence could they attain fullness of person-hood. Only in His presence could they fully expose their glory. Only in His presence could His glory shine through them.

It is important to understand the difference between the *presence* of God and the *glory* of God. Many believers today make the mistake of equating the two, when really they are quite different. The presence of God is the active manifestation of God that fills the environment in which creation exists and lives. Presence means "pre-sense"; we get a "sense" of God before He fully manifests Him-self. The presence of God is His pre-determined environment for us to function and be fruitful.

The glory of God, on the other hand, is the attributes and character of God on dis-play. While the presence of God is an envi-ronment that is very real but invisible, the glory of God is an actual, observable thing. God's glory shows us what He is like. At times His glory may be hidden but it is never invis-ible. When Moses came down from Mt. Sinai with the stone tablets containing the Ten Commandments, the Scripture says that his face was radiant because He had been in the presence of God (see Ex. 34:29-35). There was a lingering glow of divine glory on his face, something so tangible and visible that Moses donned a veil to hide it.

> **The presence of God is the active manifestation of God that fills the environment in which creation exists and lives.**

In the Garden of Eden, both the presence and the glory of God surrounded and defined the lives of the first human couple. Adam and Eve never went to a "worship service." Their worship was fellowshiping continuously with God and being everything He had created them to be. They never fasted or prayed because they were in constant communion with their Maker. They needed no Scripture to read because they were always in the presence of the living Word Himself. The presence of God has always been the conducive environment for man to be all he can be. It is the open door to everything else. We can realize our greatest potential only when we are in a full and right relationship with God. Some scholars believe that Adam and Eve did not have to wear physical clothing because they wore the manifested, tangible glory of God. They lost that glory as a result of the fall, and so now we understand better the statement in Genesis 3:7, that "they realized they were naked."

In the environment of Eden, Adam and Eve enjoyed that relationship. Equipped with everything they needed to fulfill God's purpose, they were poised on the brink of filling the earth with the glory of the Lord. What went wrong?

Trouble in Paradise

In the third chapter of Genesis, Moses records the fall of mankind from perfect relationship with God with these words:

> Now the serpent was more crafty than any of the wild animals the Lord God had made. He said to the woman, "Did God really say, 'You must not eat from any tree in the garden'?" The woman said to the serpent, "We may eat fruit from the trees in the garden, but God did say, 'You must not eat fruit from the tree that is in the middle of the garden, and you must not touch it, or you will die.'" "You will not surely die," the serpent said to the woman. "For God knows that when you eat of it your eyes will be opened, and you will be like God, knowing good and evil." When the woman saw that the fruit of the tree was good for food and pleasing to the eye, and also desirable for gaining wisdom, she took some and ate it. She also gave some to her husband, who was with her, and he ate it. Then the eyes of both of them were opened, and they realized they were

naked; so they sewed fig leaves together and made coverings for themselves (Genesis 3:1-7).

One significant characteristic of the Eden environment was freedom. Adam and Eve were created as self-determining and responsible moral beings. They were free to choose whether they would walk in the liberty of the bright path of submission and obedience to God or tread the dead-end trail of disobedience and rebellion. This freedom to choose, along with their conscious, ongoing love relationship with God, was at the very core of their being and is what made them humans instead of robots and distinguished them from the lower orders of creatures.

True freedom always comes with limits and obedience is meaningful only where standards of behavior exist. This is why God identified one particular tree in the Garden, the tree of the knowledge of good and evil, and set it off limits. It is quite possible that an alternative to submission and obedience to God never even entered the minds of Adam and Eve until the day Eve had her conversation with the adversary.

Disguised as a serpent, satan, chief of the fallen angels, that "liar and the father of lies" (Jn. 8:44b) who held "the power of death" (Heb. 2:14b), deceived and tempted Eve. Together, she and her husband traded their birthright as co-regents with their Creator for false promises of enlightenment and a quest for illegitimate glory. They surrendered their regal status to an evil pretender to the throne.

Genesis 3:7 says that after Adam and Eve ate of the forbidden fruit their eyes were opened and "they realized they were naked." This statement deals with more than just the status of their wardrobe. Until then, Adam and Eve had enjoyed the unbroken covering of the presence of God. Now, because of sin, that covering was gone and they stood apart from God, naked and exposed, cowering under the blinding glare of His holiness.

In the blink of an eye everything had changed. Gone were the warm fellowship and the joy of walks with the Lord in the Garden in the "cool of the day" (Gen. 3:8). Gone were the simple innocence and childlike trust that had characterized their relationships with each other and with God. Gone was their sense of purpose as well as their royal status. **The rulers became refugees.**

God evicted them from the Garden for their own good as well as to protect His presence. Satan and his angels had been cast out of Heaven when they threatened to contaminate it with their rebellion. Adam and Eve were cast out of Eden for the same reason. In judgment, however, there was mercy. If Adam and Eve had stayed in the Garden, they might have eaten of the tree of life and been condemned to remain forever in their fallen condition (see Gen. 3:22). Everything God does toward man is redemptive in nature. Evicting Adam and Eve from the Garden of Eden was no different. God drove them out in order to protect them and their descendants until He could bring to pass His plan to restore them to their original state.

> **E**verything God does toward man is redemptive in nature.

Counting the Cost of Rebellion

Outside the environment of God's covering presence, man cannot function properly. We were created for Eden, and apart from it we are "out of our element." What was the cost of rebellion to Adam and Eve and, through them, to the whole human race? We can best answer that question by considering two things: first, what man did *not* lose in the Fall and second, what he *did* lose. There are at least six things that man did not lose in the Fall, although the Fall did alter their quality and character.

1. *Man did not lose Heaven.* Please understand me on this. You cannot *lose* what you never *had.* Man was not

created for Heaven but for earth and, specifically, for Eden. **Heaven is the realm of God and the domain of His holy presence. Earth was the realm of man and Eden was the place where the two realms touched.** Psalm 115:16 says, "The highest heavens belong to the Lord, but the earth He has given to man." Today, we who are believers look forward to Heaven as our eternal home. Philippians 3:20 says that we are citizens of Heaven, and First Peter 1:4, that we have a spiritual inheritance kept for us in Heaven, but in the beginning we were designed for earth. Satan and his angels lost Heaven, but man did not. We did not lose Heaven because we never had Heaven to start with. The Bible begins on earth and ends on the new earth. Could it be that our "Heaven" will be the "new earth," where "the dwelling of God is with men, and He will live with them. They will be His people, and God Himself will be with them and be their God" (Rev. 21:3b)? God is going to restore that which man lost.

2. *Man did not lose the earth.* It is still our home, the environment in which we live, breathe, work, play, and die. What we *did* lose, however, is our *mastery* of the earth. No matter how much we have tamed the elements and learned to survive and even thrive in a basically hostile and threatening environment, we are no longer truly masters of the earthly domain. We have fallen far from the lordly state we enjoyed at Creation and, in this dispensation of God's redemptive work, are helpless to return to it fully.

3. *Man did not lose his spirit.* We are still spirit beings. Unlike all other creatures, we possess a spiritual nature that, whether good or bad, sinful or righteous, lives forever. This is part of the divine image of Himself that God placed inside each of us.

4. *Man did not lose his body.* Just as life in space requires a space suit, life on earth requires an "earth suit." God fashioned our physical bodies to be suited to the earth environment He prepared for us. Sin has corrupted both our bodies and the earth, so neither function as well as they should. The natural harmony that once existed between them is gone. Life in the Garden was joyous and purposeful; outside the Garden (away from God's presence) it is a difficult, often empty struggle. That which was immortal has become mortal, or death-full.

5. *Man did not lose his soul.* By "soul" I mean our full mental capacity. The soul consists of the mind, the will, and the emotions. Each of us still has a mind that thinks, emotions that feel, and a will that acts. We are conscious, independent beings with freedom of choice, just as God created us. Because of the Fall, however, we have a sin nature that causes us to make wrong choices. Our will has become a victim of our fallen, corrupt nature. Our desire is overpowered by our will. We are slaves to our sinful nature and, on our own, helpless to overcome it. Even when we desire to do the right thing, our sinful will causes us to do otherwise. The New Testament writer Paul described this dilemma perfectly when he wrote:

    I do not understand what I do. For what I want to do I do not do, but what I hate I do….As it is, it is no longer I myself who do it, but it is sin living in me. I know that nothing good lives in me, that is, in my sinful nature. For I have the desire to do what is good, but I cannot carry it out….So, I find this law at work: when I want to do good, evil is right there with me (Romans 7:15;17-18;21).

Paul goes on to say that it is only in Christ that we can find freedom from this bondage.

6. *Man did not lose his potential.* Even in our fallen state, the human race possesses enormous potential. Potential is untapped power, unused ability, unrealized dreams, unfulfilled promises. We can think of potential another way as *undisplayed glory.* God always sees in us more than we see in ourselves. I have said many times before that God sees things in us that everyone else ignores. Sin has blinded us to who we really are and what we can really be and do. We need the presence and power of God to help us bring out the potential—the glory—that lies dormant inside us.

The Lost Treasures of Man

If in the Fall man did not lose Heaven, the earth, his spirit, his body, his soul, or his potential, what *did* he lose?

1. *Man lost his purity.* The word *purity* is another word for holiness. Both words convey the idea of cleanliness, of being without spot, stain, or blemish. A related idea is that of *transparency,* meaning "no cloud or shadow of deception or falsehood." What was the first thing Adam and Eve did after they disobeyed God? They lied and tried to cover up their actions. They also tried to "pass the buck." Adam blamed Eve for giving him the fruit, and even implied that God was at fault for giving Eve to him in the first place. Eve blamed the serpent for tricking her. Loss of purity means loss of honesty and openness. It means a life characterized by lies and deception. Adam and Eve tried to cover up their sin, and humanity has been a race of "cover-ups" ever since. In contrast, purity and holiness have to do with integrity. The word *integrity,* which means "complete or undivided," is related to

the word *integrate,* which means "to unite or to form into a unified whole." In other words, integrity has to do with "oneness." Purity and holiness mean that what we say and what we do are the same thing; there is no difference between our public life and our private life. That's integrity. Another word for purity, holiness, and integrity is *glory.* That's what Adam and Eve lost. Impurity breeds hypocrisy. Before the Fall, they enjoyed perfect openness and trust in their relationships. Afterward, they were unable to be honest with God, with each other, or even with themselves.

2. *Man lost the Holy Spirit.* When Adam and Eve sinned, the personal presence of the Lord in their lives—the Holy Spirit—departed. His absence handicapped them because the knowledge, wisdom, power, gifts, and fruit that He provided, and which they had taken for granted, were gone. It became impossible for them to function properly, or to understand fully who and what they were and what they were capable of. This reality is still with us today. Without the Holy Spirit, man can never experience his full glory.

3. *Man lost Eden (the covering presence of God).* After God drove out Adam and Eve, "He placed on the east side of the Garden of Eden cherubim and a flaming sword flashing back and forth to guard the way to the tree of life" (Gen. 3:24b). The word *cherubim* is plural. The way back into Eden was guarded by at least two angels, and possibly an entire host of them. With this eviction, God accomplished two things: He protected His holy environment from sinful man's contaminating presence, and He protected sinful man from eating of the tree of life and thereby living forever in his fallen condition. By protecting them from the tree of life He protected them from eternal damnation. If

man had eaten from the tree of life in his fallen, contaminated state, it would have rendered him a permanent, eternal sinner. God in His perfect wisdom and grace protected man from his own eternal damnation and gave hope for the redemption of future generations in Adam's loins. The immediate and long-term consequence of the Fall was that man, spiritually impaired by sin, had to try to function in an environment he was not designed for. In the Garden, life was purposeful. Even the work of tending the Garden was not laborious because Adam and Eve were fulfilling their natural glory. Outside, however, the environment was hostile and resistant. Life became a continuing cycle of blood, tears, toil, and sweat.

4. *Man lost the fullness of the glory of God.* Without the covering presence of God, and without His indwelling Spirit, Adam and Eve could not even fully express their own glory, much less the glory of God. Despite sin, man still had the image of God, although it was marred and distorted. The latent glory of God in them could not come out because it was buried under the sinfulness of their fleshly nature.

5. *Man lost dominion over the earth.* Satan used trickery and deceit to induce Adam and Eve to disobey God. By their own choice they forfeited their dominion over the created order. Those who were created to rule took their crown and seal of authority and handed them over to an unemployed cherub. The true glory of the sons of men has since been buried under the confusion, ignorance, and frustration of the Fall.

6. *Man lost his sense of purpose.* As the generations passed, man quickly forgot who he was, why he was here, where he came from, and where he was going. Life

became a daily grind of fear, despair, and hopelessness. Having lost Eden, man was out of his element and malfunctioned. We have been malfunctioning ever since, struggling hard to answer those questions and to find a way back to where we once belonged. The presence of God conceals the purpose of man. Without God's presence man has no purpose, and without purpose, life is an experiment.

Lost, Restless, and Wandering

We find in the biblical account of Cain a perfect example of this lostness of man. Cain, you may recall, was the firstborn son of Adam and Eve who murdered his brother, Abel (see Gen. 4:1-8). In pronouncing judgment on Cain for his deed God said, "Now you are under a curse and driven from the ground, which opened its mouth to receive your brother's blood from your hand. When you work the ground, it will no longer yield its crops for you. You will be a restless wanderer on the earth" (Gen. 4:11-12). "A restless wanderer on the earth." That describes all of humanity since the Fall.

What effect did God's judgment have on Cain?

Cain said to the Lord, "My punishment is more than I can bear. Today You are driving me from the land, and I will be hidden from Your presence; I will be a restless wanderer on the earth, and whoever finds me will kill me." But the Lord said to him, "Not so; if anyone kills Cain, he will suffer vengeance seven times over." Then the Lord put a mark on Cain so that no one who found him would kill him. So Cain went out from the Lord's presence and lived in the land of Nod, east of Eden (Genesis 4:13-16).

Cain considered his punishment unbearable. He was filled with self-loathing. Outside of God's presence we develop a self-hatred. Faced with his loss, Cain developed a death wish. Only God's specific intervention kept it from happening. It is interesting to note that for Cain, the most unbearable thing was not death but the loss of God's presence. The rest of chapter 4 of Genesis talks about Lamech, Cain's great-great-great grandson, who was even more murderous than his ancestor. After that, Cain's family line disappears from Scripture.

Cain represents the millions of people throughout history, even to our own day, whose glory never comes out. They, like he, are "restless wanderers" on the earth, without purpose or meaning. Cain never revealed his true glory. We will never know who Cain could have become.

Protecting God's Environment

One of the biggest issues in our world today is protecting our natural environment. Ozone depletion, carbon dioxide buildup, global warming, rain forest destruction, extinction of species, and availability and quality of drinking water are foremost concerns in the minds of many people around the globe. In the past, massive oil spills from damaged supertankers have captured worldwide attention amid fear and speculation concerning their harm to the environment. The explosion and radiation leak at the Chernobyl nuclear power plant in the former Soviet Union sent shock waves of fear around the world.

Our concern for the earth's environment says two things about us. First, it reveals that we still have the spirit of dominion over the created order that God gave us in the beginning. Despite our sinful nature, we still have a proprietary interest as overlords of the earth. Second, it demonstrates what a generally poor job we have done. Ever since the Fall, we have been refugees in our own domain and in many ways have lost control of it. Now we are scrambling to get it back. Even as fallen creatures, we understand the importance of protecting our environment.

God understands the importance of protecting His environment, too. Sin made it necessary for God to remove man from His presence. God is very jealous for His name and His holiness. He protects His own environment because His nature and function require it. That is why God could not ignore sin. He had to deal with it. Sin disturbed His presence, and therefore disturbed His glory. It threatened the integrity of the entire created order. Sin was so serious to God that He sent His only Son to get rid of it by dying on the cross. God's presence is His priority and our necessity. Protecting God's presence should be our priority.

At the root of sin is willful rebellion against the known will of God. That's what Adam and Eve did. They didn't lie (at first), they didn't steal, they didn't curse, they didn't murder, they didn't commit sexual sin; they didn't do any of the things we generally think of as sin. Adam and Eve consciously and willfully rebelled against the revealed will of God. He commanded them, "Don't eat from the tree of the knowledge of good and evil." They replied, "We *will* eat from it," and they did. Their rebellion brought contamination, and God had to separate Himself from it. Anything that disrupts the presence of God should be our greatest concern.

God's judgment on Adam and Eve may seem harsh, but that's the consequences of sin. Sin is always hard, bitter, and destructive. We cannot function properly without God's presence, nor can we enter His presence while corrupted by the stain of sin. God created us in His image. He hid a part of Himself in us and bid us to manifest our true selves by revealing our dominion power, which has its source in the same power He Himself exercises as Lord of the universe. Sin made it impossible for us to accomplish our purpose because it separated us from God's presence. We can't become what He created us to be without His presence. God's Word and will must be fulfilled, however, so He began right away to carry out His plan to restore us to our proper environment.

Even as fallen sinners, we still carry God's glory around with us, hidden inside these "earthen vessels" (see 2 Cor. 4:7 KJV) that we call our bodies. Our sin retards His presence and consequently suppresses that glory and keeps it from coming out. God says, "I will do whatever is necessary to put you back in the right environment so that you can truly reflect and display My glory. I will do whatever is necessary for you to become everything I created you to be."

That process began even in the Garden of Eden itself when God told the serpent (satan), "And I will put enmity between you and the woman, and between your offspring and hers; He will crush your head, and you will strike His heel" (Gen. 3:15). God's Son, the offspring of the woman, would come and crush the head of the author of sin and the father of lies. The wages for man's sin is death, and God said, "I'll pay it." God created us to display His glory. He will do whatever He needs to do to restore us to Himself and see His glory revealed in us.

❖ PRINCIPLES ❖

1. In order to be like God, we must know God, and to know God, we must spend time in His presence.

2. Before God created man, He prepared an environment perfectly suited to him.

3. Eden represented a state of pure, complete, and unbroken fellowship between God and man.

4. God's original purpose was for Eden to be duplicated throughout the world so that His glory truly would fill the earth.

5. The presence of God is the active manifestation of God that fills the environment in which creation exists and lives.

6. Everything God does toward man is redemptive in nature.

7. Outside the environment of God's covering presence, man cannot function properly.

8. At the root of sin is willful rebellion against the known will of God.

9. God will do whatever He needs to do to restore us to Himself and see His glory revealed in us.

Chapter Three

Glory in an "Earth Suit"

"The glory of God is humanity fully alive."[1]

Every day we enjoy the benefits of someone else's glory, and most of the time we aren't even aware of it. For example, have you ever considered where the spoon came from? Think about it a minute. Sometime, somewhere, someone invented the spoon. It may seem like a little thing, but our world would be rather different without it. The spoon is the expression of someone's glory.

What would life be like without buttons? Or zippers? Someone invented those, and the world of fashion was changed forever. Even such simple items as these came about because a human being exercised his or her God-given creativity, looked at a common problem or need from a new angle, and devised an innovative solution. The

---

1. Irenaeus, *Against Heresies*, Book IV, Chapter XX. Irenaeus (c. 120-202), one of the early church fathers, was Bishop of Lyons, France, and an ardent foe of all forms of heresy against orthodox, biblical faith.

zipper, for example, is man's copy of the same mechanism by which a bird's feather functions. Individual strands of the feather interlock tightly to form a waterproof barrier that protects the bird. The separate parts of a zipper interlock in the same way. Whenever we exercise our creativity in this way, we expose some of the glory of God, who is Himself the Master Creator.

Every time we walk into a library or a bookstore, we are surrounded by glory. The bookshelves are filled with it. Underneath every dust jacket and between every set of covers is the priceless treasure of an author's exposed glory. Whenever you buy a book you are purchasing someone's glory, the cherished product of his or her time, energy, effort, and passion. By the very act of reading *this* book you are partaking of *my* glory as its author. A finished book is its author's glory exposed.

My question to you is, "Will we ever read *yours*? Will *your* glory ever be on display for others to enjoy?"

The problem with many of us today is that we don't really know who we are. We have either forgotten or simply stopped believing what the Bible says about where we came from and why we are here. Some people have never known. This ignorance of our identity and purpose as humans pervades every society and culture around the world.

Unfortunately, this is also true for many religious believers today. The adversary has been very effective in keeping us blind and deaf to the truth. Even as believers, many of us wallow daily in guilt and self-pity with little awareness of our royal heritage as God's children. Our lives are stuck in a rut and we have no inkling of the great, God-given potential within us, much less how to bring it out. Our glory is bound up, suppressed, and hidden away. Every human on earth is an undiscovered treasure chest of God's glory. Millions will die depositing their glory in the grave.

To make matters worse, many of the "pronouncements" of modern science over the past couple of centuries have helped diminish man's view of himself and his place in the universe. Many scientists tell us that compared to the infinite vastness of the cosmos we are infinitesimally small and insignificant, nothing more than the product of billions of years of random, mindless evolution. This comparison, however, proves nothing. While it is true that anyone who takes the time to ponder the heavens can end up feeling tiny and unimportant, we need to remember that physical size has never been an accurate measure of true worth.

A Little Lower Than God

One of the greatest expressions of the dignity, worth, and place of man in the universe came not from a scientist or a great intellectual thinker, but from a humble shepherd-king from the hills of Judah in ancient Israel. As a shepherd, David must have spent many nights contemplating the heavens above him. The Bible tells us that David was a man after God's own heart (see 1 Sam. 13:14; Acts 13:22), which means that his heart and mind were in tune with God. Because of this intimate relationship, David was sensitive to divine revelation, by which he was able to give a matchless description of man's relationship with God and the rest of creation.

O Lord, our Lord, How majestic is Your name in all the earth, who have displayed Your splendor above the heavens!...When I consider Your heavens, the work of Your fingers, the moon and the stars, which You have ordained; what is man that You take thought of him, and the son of man that You care for him? Yet You have made him a little lower than God, and You crown him with glory and majesty! You make him to rule over the works of Your hands; You have put all things under his feet, all sheep and oxen, and also the beasts of the field, the birds of the heavens and the fish of the sea, whatever passes through the paths of the seas (Psalm 8:1;3-8 NAS).

When David considered the heavens he was impressed not with the smallness of man but with the greatness of God. *Splendor* is another word for glory, and David describes that splendor as the "work of [God's] fingers." Glory is tangible and observable. David's question, "What is man...?" indicates that he recognized humanity's apparent smallness against the backdrop of creation. His next statement, however, reveals that he understood man's true place in God's order: "Yet You have made him a little lower than God, and You crown him with glory and majesty!"

What an incredible statement! God created man "a little lower" than Himself! That's something that is never said even about the angels. Some translations of the Bible, such as the King James, render the phrase "a little lower than the angels." However, the Hebrew word is *elohim*, which is the most basic Old Testament word meaning "god," or "a god." *Elohim* is plural in form, and as such usually refers to God Himself. In some contexts it does refer to angels or lower "gods" such as the false gods worshiped by Israel's neighbors. In the context of Psalm 8, however, translating *elohim* as "God" makes more sense. It is the same word that is used in Genesis 1:1, "In the beginning God (*elohim*) created the heavens and the earth."

God created man in His own image. He imparted to us some of His nature, His character, and His attributes. He created us to be like Him. Nowhere in Scripture is this said about the angels. Angels were created as servants, to do God's bidding and carry out His commands. They were not given dominion over anything. Man, on the other hand, was given dominion over the earth and all life on it. God created us a "little lower" than Himself, then He "crowned" us with "glory and majesty." The Hebrew word *atar* ("crowned") is used most often, as here, in a figurative sense to show honor and authority.[2] God created us to rule, then gave us the power and authority to do it. "Glory" here is the Hebrew *kabod*, the same word used in many other places to refer to God's glory, weightiness, and splendor. "Majesty" translates the Hebrew word *hadar*, which is a

---

2.   R. Laird Harris et al., ed., *Theological Wordbook of the Old Testament*, Vol. 2 (Chicago, IL: Moody Press, 1980), p. 662.

synonym for "glory" and "honor" and also means "magnificence," "beauty," and "comeliness" (Strong's, H1926).

David understood the high estate of man in God's design. Psalm 8 describes man in his ideal innocence. It is a picture of "humanity fully alive," as the early church father Irenaeus said, ruling in majesty over the created order. It is a picture of man as he was created to be; man before the Fall.

Exchanging God's Glory for Worthless Idols

By creation and design we are carriers of God's glory; the Fall hasn't changed that. Because of the Fall, however, we are not functioning according to our design. The human race has been malfunctioning ever since Eden. Sin tarnished, marred, and distorted God's image in us and broke our relationship with Him. As a result, we lost sight of who we are and who God is.

One of the most obvious signs of this loss of identity is the countless and fruitless ways that people throughout history have attempted to satisfy their spiritual yearnings. When we no longer know who God is, we begin to worship all sorts of things that are not gods at all: images made of wood, stone, or metal, and fashioned in the shape of goats, cats, bulls, or any number of other things. Throughout the ages people have worshiped creatures rather than the Creator.

An idol is anything that we place more importance on or give more allegiance to than we do God. It could be material possessions, sports, money, a job, another person—anything that takes a higher place in our lives than God. Whenever we worship idols we prostrate both our glory and the glory of God within us before unworthy things. It's bad enough when the human race as a whole rejects the true God in favor of false gods, but it's even worse when those who are supposed to be God's special people do the same thing! Nothing grieves or angers God more. For example, despite everything God had done for them by loving them, delivering them from slavery in Egypt, and bringing them into the Promised Land, the nation of Israel repeatedly turned away from God to follow idols. As a result,

> **The Lord saw this and rejected them because He was angered by His sons and daughters. "I will hide My face from them," He said, "and see what their end will be; for they are a perverse generation, children who are unfaithful. They made Me jealous by what is no god and angered Me with their worthless idols"** (Deuteronomy 32:19-21a).

Psalm 106 describes a similar situation that occurred while the Israelites were in the desert and Moses was alone with God on the mountain, receiving the Ten Commandments:

> **At Horeb they made a calf and worshiped an idol cast from metal. They exchanged their Glory for an image of a bull, which eats grass** (Psalm 106:19-20).

The Israelites turned to "worthless idols" and "exchanged their Glory"—the image, character, and attributes of God that were in them—for the "image of a bull." They traded the glory of God and their relationship as His special people for a gold statue of a calf, one of the lesser creatures. Only the direct, personal intercession of Moses kept God from destroying the people for their great sin (see Ex. 32:7-14).

One of the reasons God hates idolatry is because it goes against His nature. Worshiping idols violates both the first commandment, "You shall have no other gods before Me" (Ex. 20:3), and the second, "You shall not make for yourself an idol in the form of anything in heaven above or on the earth beneath or in the waters below" (Ex. 20:4). God has said, in effect, "You are carriers of My image. I bow to no one. Don't *ever* bow My image before any idol of wood, stone, or metal! How dare you?"

Yet, that is exactly what the Israelites did. In the Book of Jeremiah, God challenges them over their disobedience and rejection of Him. You can almost hear the incredulity in His voice:

> **This is what the Lord says: "What fault did your fathers find in Me, that they strayed so far from Me? They followed worthless idols and became worthless themselves....Cross over to the coasts of Kittim and look, send to Kedar and observe closely; see if there has ever been anything like this: Has a nation ever changed its gods? (Yet they are not gods at all.) But My people have exchanged their Glory for worthless idols"** (Jeremiah 2:5;10-11).

Another reason God hates idolatry is because it goes against our *original* nature, the nature we had at Creation. Whenever we bow before an idol, not only are we worshiping something that is lower than God, we are worshiping something that is lower than *ourselves*. In all creation there is no higher being than man. We alone were created in God's image. Why then should we bow down to a lower creature or an inanimate object, or even an angel, thereby shaming not only our own glory, but also God's as well?

"I Will Not Give My Glory to Another"

One of the big problems with this whole issue of exposing or displaying God's glory, or fulfilling our glory as believers, is that many of us have been taught from the beginning that we *have* no glory. How often have you heard someone say, "Now watch out, brother, you've got to stay humble. Don't take the glory." What they mean is that no matter how well you exercise your gift or talent for the Lord, you should *never* say that it was you who did it. Instead, say it was the Lord. No matter how well you play the piano, paint a picture, design a home, or create a product, don't ever say that it was you who did it. Otherwise, you'll be stealing God's glory.

That's ridiculous! Of course it was you who did it! God may have given you the talent, but it was you who sat down at the keyboard and made beautiful music. It was you who put on canvas the picture that was already complete in your mind. It was you who drew up the blueprints for that new house being built down the street. Humility is very important, and we should never take credit for something that God did, but acknowledging our God-given gifts and exercising them without shame or apology is *not* stealing God's glory. On the contrary, it is a way of *giving* Him glory. We honor God by developing and using for His glory the traits, attributes, gifts, and abilities He has placed in us, being careful always to acknowledge Him as their source.

True humility means to recognize our roots. The words *humility* and *humble* are both related to the Latin word *humus,* which means "earth." Humus is the organic component of soil, consisting of partially decomposed plant or animal matter. By creation we are children of the soil in the sense that God "formed [us] from the dust of the ground and breathed into [us] the breath of life" (Gen. 2:7). Ours is an earthly glory, but our Creator has given us a god-like nature—His own.

True humility is recognizing and acknowledging who we really are: spiritual, godly beings in an earthly body. To deny our gifts and our glory is an insult to God. It is a form of false humility that has suppressed the spirits of countless Christians for generations, leaving them feeling weak, useless, and insignificant.

> **A**cknowledging our God-given gifts and exercising them without shame or apology is *not* stealing God's glory. On the contrary, it is a way of *giving* Him glory.

For years preachers, pastors, and other spiritual leaders and teachers have fostered this false attitude and passed it on to their congregations, basing it on a misunderstanding of a Scripture verse in Isaiah where God says, "I will not give My glory to another." Let's consider the context and fuller meaning of that passage.

> **This is what God the Lord says—He who created the heavens and stretched them out, who spread out the earth and all that comes out of it, who gives breath to its people, and life to those who walk on it: "I, the Lord, have called you in righteousness; I will take hold of your hand. I will keep you and will make you to be a covenant for the people and a light for the Gentiles, to open eyes that are blind, to free captives from prison and to release from the dungeon those who sit in darkness. I am the Lord; that is My name! I will not give My glory to another or My praise to idols. See, the former things have taken place, and new things I declare; before they spring into being I announce them to you"** (Isaiah 42:5-9).

These verses comprise a portion of one of a sequence of four "servant songs" in the Book of Isaiah, so called because they refer to a Spirit-filled "servant" whom God will send to "bring justice to the nations" (Is. 42:1). The New Testament identifies this servant as Jesus Christ (see Matt. 12:15-21). In the passage above, God is addressing the nation of Israel, the people through whom Christ would come. His words refer to the original purpose behind His raising up of the Jewish nation, that they would be "a covenant for the people and a light for the Gentiles, to open eyes that are blind, to free captives from prison and to release from the dungeon those who sit in darkness." To this end, the Israelites were to love, worship, and serve God and Him only.

Instead, the people repeatedly rejected God and turned away from Him, following false gods and falling into gross idolatry and immorality. They bowed down to images of wood, stone, and metal, and offered up sacrifices to them. God judged the nation by delivering them into the hands of the Babylonians for 70 years.

❖ The Glory of Living

Isaiah 42:18-25 is a prophecy of this captivity, announced years before it happened.

With the prophecies of both the coming servant and the coming judgment, God wanted His people to know beyond doubt that it was He and not their idols who was the one true God and that it was He who held the future and could therefore predict it. In righteous and holy anger at their unfaithfulness, God declared, "I am the Lord; that is My name! I will not give My glory to another or My praise to idols." He would not sit idly by while His people attributed His works, His glory, His name, and His character to blocks of wood and slabs of stone. God would not allow His glory to be given to man-made images of created beings.

There is another aspect to this as well. I believe that when God said, "I will not give My glory to another," He meant not only that He would not permit His works and His character to be credited to idols, but also that He would not permit His people, the carriers of His glory, to prostrate His image before them. Of all God's creatures, man alone was made in His image. To us alone did God bestow part of His nature, His attributes, and His glory. He is saying to us, "I gave My glory to *you*. I will not give it to another creature. Why should you who carry My glory bow down before the likeness of a creature that possesses neither My image nor My glory? Are you crazy?"

In our modern world, at least in the West, there are probably few people today who physically bow and worship before idols of wood or stone. That's not really the point. The central issue here is not the physical position of the body but the spiritual position of the heart. Anytime we allow anyone or anything to take a higher place in our life than God, we are guilty of "giving His glory to another." That's idolatry, no matter what form it takes. We were made to be masters of our environment, not slaves of it.

Life Inside an "Earth Suit"

The story is told of a man who bought a cheap painting for a few dollars at a flea market. Upon examining it closer after he got it home, he discovered that the canvas appeared to be much older than the painting itself. Further inspection of the picture revealed that it had been painted over another, much older work of art. The cheaper, more recent painting was carefully removed and stripped away until the older work underneath was uncovered. Upon appraisal, the older painting was determined to be an original work by a great European master artist, and was valued at several million dollars. No one knew the true value—the glory—that lay beneath until that which concealed it was taken away.

Like the man from the flea market who was determined to reveal the true glory of the painting he possessed, God wants us to share and display His glory. Too often, however, no one can see it in our lives because it is buried beneath our intimidation and fear, our discouragement, our bad attitudes, and the negative thoughts and opinions we have built up in our minds over the years. God's glory in us can't shine forth because of all the junk of the world that we have piled on top of it. Somehow we've got to dig away the dirt and debris of our drab daily existence and uncover the treasure of divine glory hidden underneath. We've got to learn how to take these fragile "jars of clay" that are our bodies and turn them into "goblets of glory."

Some of us have believed for so long that we have no glory that it's hard to change our thinking. The apostle Paul, however, had a solid handle on the idea.

Now to Him who is able to do immeasurably more than all we ask or imagine, according to His power that is at work within us, to Him be glory in the church and in Christ Jesus throughout all generations, for ever and ever! Amen (Ephesians 3:20-21).

❖ The Glory of Living

Paul speaks of the immeasurable power of God that is at work where? *Within us!* God's glory is where? *In the Church!* And what is the Church? *A body of believers, a worldwide community consisting of every follower of Christ!* In other words, God's power and glory reside inside each of us who knows Jesus Christ as Savior and Lord!

For God, who said, "Let light shine out of darkness," made His light shine in our hearts to give us the light of the knowledge of the glory of God in the face of Christ. But we have this treasure in jars of clay to show that this all-surpassing power is from God and not from us. We are hard pressed on every side, but not crushed; perplexed, but not in despair; persecuted, but not abandoned; struck down, but not destroyed. We always carry around in our body the death of Jesus, so that the life of Jesus may also be revealed in our body (2 Corinthians 4:6-10).

As believers, we have in our hearts the "light of the knowledge of the glory of God," who put it there. It is a "treasure" that we carry around in fragile "jars of clay"— our physical bodies. God wants that light to shine brightly in the midst of a dark world. For many of us, our "jars of clay" are very ordinary looking, perhaps even unimpressive; not the kind of vessel in which anyone would expect to find treasure. It would be like concealing a diamond in a shoebox. God's power at work in us is much greater than anything we could ever do by ourselves, so that when people look at us they will see Him. They will see working in our lives something that only God can do. God will be on display in our lives and in this way we will bring glory to His name.

> **We've got to learn how to take these fragile "jars of clay" that are our bodies and turn them into "goblets of glory."**

We are walking, talking treasure chests, and God does not want us to take that treasure with us to the grave. He didn't place His glory in us for it to end up buried and dormant in a cemetery! His desire is for us to give full expression to the glory that resides within us. God hid His "treasure" inside our "jars of clay," but He doesn't want it to stay there. He wants us to show off what's hidden inside so that people everywhere will know "that this all-surpassing power is from God and not from us." We should live in such a way that people who have been around us will say, "There is no doubt about it, God was here!" We should live so close to the Lord that when people look at us they will see Him shining out of our lives. If we really become and do what God called us to be and do, His glory will shine forth and people will know that God has been on earth in an "earth suit."

The Glory of Productivity

Psalm 19:1 says, "The heavens declare the glory of God; the skies proclaim the work of his hands." We also are the work of His hands. Just as God's glory is displayed in "the work of His hands," so He has created us to display His glory by the work we do. In Ephesians 2:10 the apostle Paul writes, "For we are God's workmanship, created in Christ Jesus to do good works, which God prepared in advance for us to do." From the very beginning God had in mind that we would do good works in the name and power of Jesus Christ, and thereby display His glory in all the earth. We have a responsibility before God to be faithful in the tasks He places before us, because He does not want us to take our gifts, talents, and abilities to the grave unused. The wise man in Ecclesiastes gives us good counsel here: "Whatever your hand finds to do, do it with all your might, for in the grave, where you are going, there is neither working nor planning nor knowledge nor wisdom" (Eccles. 9:10). **God did not create us to do nothing.** He has endowed us with intelligence, creativity, spiritual gifts, and natural abilities, and He expects us to use them, to pour them out in service to others for the glory of His name.

❖ **The Glory of Living**

God did not create us to make a living, but to show the world what He is like. Our glory is to give full expression to everything God created us to be and do. It's time to learn how to tap into our glory—to find our full expression. We need to bring out all the ideas, the plans, and the dreams that are buried inside us. God put them there in order that we might fulfill them and give them life, and body, and character. We cannot do this in our own strength or wisdom; it calls for God's power. However, God "is able to do immeasurably more than all we ask or imagine, according to His power that is at work within us" (Eph. 3:20).

God created us to be creative just as He is creative. No other creature has this capacity. When we exercise our creativity we are displaying the God-like attributes and nature He placed in us. That's why most of the time we don't really glorify God in a church service, because we aren't "doing" anything. We're not working or "creating" anything. It's when we go home and start planning our week that the glory begins to come out. God is glorified when we find creative ways to give full expression to His nature and attributes and to the life of Christ that dwells within us. Whether it's taking some risks, trying bold new ventures, stepping out to attempt things we have never done before, building a business, making wise investments, or seeking new and innovative ways to share the gospel of Christ effectively, God's glory comes out when we follow His Spirit and depend on His power to become everything He means for us to be.

When we exercise our creativity we are displaying the God-like attributes and nature He placed in us.

We display our glory when we reveal the glory of God in us, both by faithfully proclaiming the message of Christ to the world whenever and however we can, and by the works of our hands in day-to-day life. When we begin showing the glory of God in our lives, He comes in and does more than we could ever plan or expect. We find our glory in becoming everything God created us to be.

❖ PRINCIPLES ❖

1. God created us a "little lower" than Himself.

2. An idol is anything that we place more importance on or give more allegiance to than we do God.

3. Whenever we bow before an idol, not only are we worshiping something that is lower than God, we are worshiping something that is lower than ourselves.

4. Acknowledging our God-given gifts and exercising them without shame or apology is *not* stealing God's glory. On the contrary, it is a way of *giving* Him glory.

5. God will not allow His glory to be given to man-made idols.

6. God will not allow His people, the carriers of His glory, to prostrate His image before idols.

7. We've got to learn how to take these fragile "jars of clay" that are our bodies and turn them into "goblets of glory."

8. We should live so close to the Lord that when people look at us they will see Him shining out of our lives.

9. God does not want us to take our gifts, talents, and abilities to the grave unused.

10. When we exercise our creativity we are displaying the God-like attributes and nature He placed in us.

11. God is glorified when we find creative ways to give full expression to His nature and attributes and to the life of Christ that dwells within us.

❖ **The Glory of Living**

12. We find our glory in becoming everything God created us to be.

Chapter Four

The Glory of "Becoming"

**" 'Tis God gives skill,
but not without men's hands: He could not make
Antonio Stradivari's violins
without Antonio."[1]**

Would you purchase a $3000 computer and then drop it in the first garbage can you found? "What a silly question!" you would say to me. "Of course not. That would be ridiculous!" A brand-new computer in a garbage can is useless. All the potential built into it by its manufacturer is still there, but there is no way to bring it out. You can't plug it in because it's in the wrong environment. Without electricity it has no source of power. All that potential, but—useless! How disappointing! How tragic! Even more tragic,

---

1. George Eliot [Marian Evans Cross], *Stradivarius*, quoted in John Bartlett, *Bartlett's Familiar Quotations*, 16th ed., Justin Kaplan, ed. (New York: Little, Brown and Company, 1992), p. 483:6.

however, is the fact that every day treasure much more valuable than this is cast onto the streets and garbage dumps of the world.

Once, when I was ministering in **Oaxaca, Mexico**, I witnessed for myself one of the heartbreaking tragedies of that great city: **30,000 children living on a huge garbage dump**. These children are the refuse of society, with little hope, few prospects, and nowhere else to go.

In Rio de Janeiro **three million children live on the streets!** Half a world away, massive poverty, starvation, and the scourge of AIDS are decimating the populations of many African nations. Young adults and children in particular are among the hardest hit. Many other nations of the earth, particularly third-world countries, share similar grim statistics.

Society has dumped glory on the garbage heap! Glory has been abandoned on the streets, and left destitute in the dirt! Will we ever see the glory in these children? Will they ever have the chance to bring out their full potential? The sad truth is that many of them—perhaps most—will die before reaching adulthood and without ever discovering who they really are. They will go to the grave never knowing who they could have become or what they might have achieved. What a terrible loss to the world! **Premature termination is the death of potential, and the death of potential is the destruction of glory.** Millions of people die every day, taking their glory with them to the grave.

The Grave of Glory

I have said many times before that the wealthiest spot on earth is not the diamond minds of South Africa, or the oil fields of South America, but the cemetery. Graveyards all over the world are great repositories of lost treasure: unwritten books, unpainted paintings, uncomposed music, unpenned poetry, unrealized dreams, unfulfilled hopes, unexpressed ideas, unreleased potential, and unfinished growth. Every day thousands of people go to their graves without ever having revealed their true or full glory.

Remember that one definition of glory is the full expression of the true nature of a thing. Tragically, many people die and never fully express who they were. Just as tragically, they take with them all the positive contributions they could have made to human society and to God's purposes in the world but didn't. Whether due to poverty, ignorance, oppression, illness, spiritual blindness, procrastination, or just plain disobedience, multitudes of people either fail or never have the opportunity to fully become everything God meant for them to be. They take all their hopes and dreams to the grave and their glory dies with them.

As long as we are alive the possibility exists for us to reach our full potential. God has endowed us with gifts, talents, and abilities, and He wants us to use them for His glory and for mankind's good. We should strive to freely pour out all that is in us in unselfish service to the world. If we fully express ourselves in this life as God desires, we will not take any unfulfilled potential with us to the grave. Our goal should be to "die empty."

Yet many of us, even as believers, wonder if we really have anything to offer. If we get down to the heart of the matter, we often secretly doubt that we can be of any use whatsoever to God. Ignorance, unbelief, erroneous teaching, and the monotonous grind of daily life blind us to our potential. God wants us to look at ourselves and our place in the world from His perspective. He wants us to see through His eyes.

When the southern kingdom of Judah was conquered by the Babylonians in 586 B.C. and God's people were taken into exile, they may have thought their usefulness to God was finished. After all, they had been unfaithful to Him and He had judged them. Their nation had fallen and Jerusalem and the temple had been destroyed. From their perspective any potential they had once had was pretty well shot. God, however, saw things differently. In the midst of the lowest point in their history, God revealed that He was not through with them yet.

> **This is what the Lord says: "When seventy years are completed for Babylon, I will come to you and fulfill My gracious promise to bring you back to this place. For I know the plans I have for you," declares the Lord, "plans to prosper you and not to harm you, plans to give you hope and a future. Then you will call upon Me and come and pray to Me, and I will listen to you. You will seek Me and find Me when you seek Me with all your heart. I will be found by you," declares the Lord, "and will bring you back from captivity. I will gather you from all the nations and places where I have banished you," declares the Lord, "and will bring you back to the place from which I carried you into exile"** (Jeremiah 29:10-14).

No matter who we are, where we come from, where we have been, or what we have done, God has plans to "prosper" us and give us "hope and a future." He has the power and the desire to bring us back from whatever "captivity" we are in that prevents us from fulfilling the potential He has placed in us. Our part is to seek Him, believe Him, trust Him, and obey Him.

Work Is "Becoming" to Man

In our modern society, when someone has achieved success in a career or endeavor, it is common to say that person has "arrived." For most of us, the world has not "seen" us yet; we have not yet "arrived." We are still in the process of becoming. Some of us are farther along than others, and some have barely begun the journey. It's important to remember that God views success differently than the world does. To the world, success equates to wealth, power, and influence. Godly success, while it may include any or all of these elements, focuses not on the outward but on the inward. God looks at the heart. We are successful in God's eyes when we live and walk in obedience to His will, work out His calling in our lives, and devote our time and energy to becoming the people He wants us to be. **Godly success is fully exposing the glory within us.**

Although it often is hidden, glory is tangible and observable. Our glory is revealed in our activity: in the "fleshing out" of our dreams, thoughts, and ideas, and in the works of our hands under the leadership of the Holy Spirit. To accomplish the full expression of glory requires the correct environment. For man, that environment is Eden, which is the presence of God. God wants to restore the original environment of Eden.

> **Now the Lord God had planted a garden in the east, in Eden; and there He put the man He had formed. And the Lord God made all kinds of trees grow out of the ground—trees that were pleasing to the eye and good for food. In the middle of the garden were the tree of life and the tree of the knowledge of good and evil....The Lord God took the man and put him in the Garden of Eden to work it and take care of it** (Genesis 2:8-9;15).

God put Adam in the Garden to do what? *To work it and take care of it.* He didn't put Adam there to sing songs or hold prayer meetings. God put him there to *work.* There was no need for worship songs or prayer in the Garden because Adam enjoyed unbroken worship and fellowship with God 24 hours a day. Adam's assignment to "work" the Garden added fullness, purpose, enrichment, and meaning to his life.

In Genesis 2:15 the word *work* translates the Hebrew word *abad.* It is the same word that is used in Genesis 2:5, "...and there was no man to *work* the ground." *Abad* appears to stem from several ancient Semitic roots: an Aramaic root that means "to do or make," an Arabic root that means "to worship, obey," and a related stem that means "to enslave, reduce to servitude."[2] The biblical concept of work, then, involves creativity, worship, obedience, and service.

---

2. R. Laird Harris et al., ed., *Theological Wordbook of the Old Testament,* Vol. 2 (Chicago, IL: Moody Press, 1980), p. 639.

❖ The Glory of Living

In these meanings we can see the full range of what "work" meant for Adam in the Garden. First, Adam exercised his God-given creativity by cultivating it; by "doing" things to help "make" the Garden flourish. Second, Adam's work was his service to God. It was "servitude," but not in any negative sense. On the contrary, such service to God was "not bondage, but rather a joyous and liberating experience."[3] It was joyous and liberating because Adam was being what he was created to be. Work as service also means to serve oneself to the world; to pour out, expend, express, and expose one's fullest energy and potential for the good and benefit of others. Third, when Adam worked he was obeying God, and in this he experienced worship. In the Garden, Adam's work *was* his worship! How often do we think of *our* work as our worship?

The Hebrew word for "take care of" in Genesis 2:15 is *shamar,* which means "to keep," or "to guard or protect." It also is used to mean "watchman" (Strong's H8104). Adam was not only the caretaker of the Garden, but also its guardian, protector, and watchman. I find it interesting to note that in Genesis 3:24, where God drives Adam and Eve from the Garden and places "cherubim and a flaming sword flashing back and forth to guard the way to the tree of life," that the same Hebrew word *shamar* is used for "guard." God had to assign cherubim to carry out a responsibility originally assigned to Adam, who was no longer fit for it!

Adam found his purpose—his glory—in the work God appointed to him as caretaker and guardian of the Garden. As long as he focused his attention on God and on the work God had given him to do, Adam was fulfilled and was able to express his full potential. Work was "becoming" for Adam; it was what he was created for. God created Adam and put him to work in the Garden so that he could become the full person God intended him to be. Work is self-expression. As man is the image and glory of God, his work is the expression and exposure of God's glory and nature.

---

3. Harris, *Theological Wordbook of the Old Testament.*

Find What You Were Born to Do

God created us to find satisfaction in our work within the framework of a personal love relationship with Him through Christ. Seeing ourselves through God's eyes is the only way we can know the person we really are. Finding purposeful, meaningful work is essential for understanding and becoming that person. Once we come to know who we are from God's perspective, we are better able to recognize the work for which He has prepared us and to which He has called us.

That is why our society is so full of dissatisfied people. Many persons, including many believers, live unfulfilled lives because they are stuck in jobs they hate or in careers they are unsuited for, either by temperament or by training. They are frustrated and discouraged because the work they do day by day actually helps prevent them from realizing their dreams. These people are not becoming who they were born to be because they are not doing what they were born to do.

Are you one of them? Do you go to work every day wishing you were somewhere else doing something else? Does your current job hinder you from becoming what you believe God wants you to be? Does it suppress your potential and keep you from letting out your true self—from exposing your glory? If so, then it is very possible that you are not where you are supposed to be. It may be that you have not yet "found your calling."

Caution is in order, however. If these things are true of you, don't just abruptly quit your job. Be careful to seek God's direction first. It may be that He is allowing you to spend some time "in the wilderness" while He builds patience and character in your life in preparation for greater things. Moses spent 40 years in Pharaoh's court and another 40 years as a shepherd in the desert of Midian before he was ready for the work to which God had called him: leading the Israelites out of slavery in Egypt. You may be going through a "dry" period while God prepares to bring you into your "season."

How can we know whether it's time to move on or to "hang tough" for awhile? That's where the personal love relationship with God comes in. The closer we walk with the Lord, and the more time we spend in His Word and in His presence, the easier it will be for us to hear His voice and know what He wants us to do.

I have an architect friend who absolutely comes alive whenever anyone begins talking about designs and developing ideas. It's obvious to everyone that he loves his work. Being an architect is his gift; he has found his true calling. My friend gets a real charge out of designing and creating things that never existed before. He thrives on it.

Yet there are some architects who hate going to work because architecture is not really their gift. They may have become architects in order to please their mother or their father. They may have been motivated only by the desire for money and a "successful" career, but their heart is not really in it. The same could be said of many people in any career or profession, whether it is medicine, law, business, engineering, or whatever. Fulfillment eludes them because they are trying to live out their parents' dream rather than their own, or pursuing a false vision of success rather than pursuing God's purpose.

God has no desire to see us go through life searching vainly for our purpose, finding it only after we retire (if then); He wants us to know it now. We should heed the words of the "Teacher" in Ecclesiastes:

> **Remember your Creator in the days of your youth, before the days of trouble come and the years approach when you will say, "I find no pleasure in them"—....Remember Him—before the silver cord is severed, or the golden bowl is broken; before the pitcher is shattered at the spring, or the wheel broken at the well, and the dust**

returns to the ground it came from, and the spirit returns to God who gave it (Ecclesiastes 12:1;6-7).

God has a purpose for each of us, a role to play in His cosmic drama of redemption for a lost world. Your role will be different from mine and, indeed, from that of anyone else. We are each unique. **God has ordained a part for you that you alone can play.** The tragedy is that so many people never discover their part until after the curtain call. God calls us to turn to Him for guidance. "Trust in the Lord with all your heart and lean not on your own understanding; in all your ways acknowledge Him, and He will make your paths straight" (Prov. 3:5-6). Another way to render that last phrase is "He will direct your paths."

If we trust God and obey His will, He will bring us "onstage" at just the right time to play the "role of a lifetime"—a role He has been preparing us for all along. Then we will be able to say with the psalmist, "For you have been my hope, O Sovereign Lord, my confidence since my youth….Since my youth, O God, you have taught me, and to this day I declare your marvelous deeds" (Ps. 71:5,17).

There is no competition when it comes to glory. Our roles may all be different, but our purpose is the same: to glorify God. The "Teacher" in Ecclesiastes sums it up well:

Now all has been heard; here is the conclusion of the matter: Fear God and keep His commandments, for this is the whole duty of man (Ecclesiastes 12:13).

Seeds of Glory

I think one of the best ways to describe this process of "becoming" is with the analogy of a seed. Take an apple seed for example. At first glance, an apple seed doesn't look like much; it's small, brown, and hard. Many people wouldn't give it a second thought. An orchardist, however, would immediately recognize its worth. The value of an apple seed is found not so much in what it is but in what it can become. An apple seed is just a seed, but hidden inside is the potential to become an apple tree and even an entire orchard of apple trees.

This is not an automatic process. Having the apple seed does not guarantee the apple tree. In a sense, the tree is already in the seed; God put it there. That's the potential—the glory—of the seed. Before the apple seed can realize its full potential and become an apple tree it must be planted in the proper environment where it can be nurtured and cared for. When all the conditions are right—fertile soil, irrigation, the proper climate, and plenty of sunshine—the seed will sprout and produce a tree. It's inevitable. That's the way God designed it. The apple seed will fully express its glory and the result will be a tree that is "heavy" (as in *kabod*, "glory") with crisp, juicy apples. The apple seed will have "become" what God intended it to be: an apple tree bursting with fruit.

That's how God works. He always sees beyond the obvious. He looks past what *is* to what *can be*. God programmed growth and maturity into every living thing He created. When God promised a son to Abraham, He did not look at a 75-year-old man who was past the age for fathering children but focused instead on the *nation* of people that would descend from him. This was part of God's plan. Abraham's body contained the potential for a multitude of descendants, but he had to follow God in faith. Abraham's love relationship with God and his obedience formed the environment that made it possible for him to release his potential. The writer of Hebrews summed it up this way: "And so from this one man, and he as good as dead, came descendants as numerous as the stars in the sky and as countless as the sand on the seashore" (Heb. 11:12). Abraham began with only a "seed of glory" but ended up "becoming" the father of a nation.

Today there are many of us who are not "becoming" the people we really are inside. This is either because we are in the wrong environment or because we are not giving proper nourishment to the "seeds of glory" that are hidden within us. In order for those

"seeds" to sprout and flourish we need the nurturing environment of the presence of God. In a sense, we need to return to
Eden. Choices we make every day affect both the environment in
which we live and breathe and the growth and health of the "tree"
of glory in us that wants to come out. How we spend our time,
what we spend our money on, what we feed our bodies, the ideas
and images that fill our minds from books, movies, television, or
the Internet; all of these are factors in determining whether our
"tree" will be healthy, or whether it will be stunted, deformed, and
malnourished.

All of us have at least an idea of the treasures inside us. That's
why we have dreams and ambitions. **God has planted in us dreams,
ideas, passions, imagination, creativity, and hope. These things
require the right environment in order to flourish and come to
fruition.** "Eden" is the only environment that is truly suitable. God
designed us for Eden and there alone can we reach our full potential. It is only when we are in the "garden of God's presence" that
we can "become."

Don't Die in the Seed

Premature death aborts glory. Children who die before reaching maturity never reveal the fullness of who they could have been.
They "die in the seed." In our world today we face a deadly "glory
conspiracy," a scheme concocted by the adversary to destroy human
glory before it is manifested. We see the evidence of this conspiracy most clearly in the prevalence of abortion.

I was visiting in a hospital one day when I observed a doctor
leaving the pregnancy ward. In his hand was a metal pail containing the remains of an aborted fetus. It was a heart wrenching sight!
Yet, that scene is replayed over and over millions of times every day
in thousands of hospitals and abortion clinics all over the world. We
will never see the glory of these children. Their treasures are lost to
the world forever. This is not God's design.

❖ The Glory of Living

The glory of a boy is the man; the glory of a girl is the woman. Glory is the true essence and nature of a thing. The true essence and nature of a boy or a girl is the man or woman they are to become. Just as a seed must "die" in order to bring forth the tree, so the boy must "die" for the man to emerge. The girl must "die" before the woman can appear. A boy cannot become a man and remain a boy. A girl cannot grow into a woman and remain a girl. One must give way to the other. This is the natural process of growth and maturity, the natural goal of glory.

Life is an unbroken process of "becoming." **Whoever we were born to be we already are, but bringing it out requires patience, hard work, and the right environment.** So, how do we bring out the full glory within us?

Being in the proper environment is the most important thing. No amount of patience and hard work will produce a good result if we're trying to work in the wrong place or at the wrong task. Look at the sequence in Genesis: first, God placed Adam in the Garden of Eden, *then* He assigned him work to do. The location was more important than the command. **Where we are is more important than what we're doing.** If we're in the wrong place, we'll never accomplish what we're supposed to do or become who we're supposed to be. This is true whether we're talking about our career or our spiritual walk as believers.

Living in a growing love relationship with God is more important than anything *we* could try to do for Him. He wants us in relationship with Him before anything else. We tend to become like the people we spend the most time with. If we want to become like God and bring out His glory within us, we need to "hang out" with Him. That's why living and working in the environment of His presence is so important.

Glory is the fullness of maturity exposed. Jesus said, "Be perfect, therefore, as your heavenly Father is perfect" (Matt. 5:48). The word *perfect* (Gk. *teleios*) means "completeness," or "of full age"

(Strong's G5046). *Perfect* here does not mean "without defect," at least in relation to man. God truly is perfect, but we are not. *Perfect* means "complete." Another word for it is maturity. There is no such thing as a perfect person, but there is such a thing as a complete person, a fully mature person.

It is a tragedy for something to die before it has a chance to reach full maturity. **If an apple tree dies in the seed, we never see its glory. God does not want us to die in seed form.** He filled us with His glory in order that we might pour it out before men, thereby revealing to the world His Person and His eternal purpose.

Glorifying God means releasing our full potential. We do this in two ways: by the work we do every day and by pursuing a life of personal holiness. We glorify God in our work not only in the nature of that work but in the attitude we take toward it. Remember the words of the "Teacher": "Whatever your hand finds to do, do it with all your might" (Eccles. 9:10a). In his letter to the Colossians Paul wrote, "Whatever you do, work at it with all your heart, as working for the Lord, not for men, since you know that you will receive an inheritance from the Lord as a reward. It is the Lord Christ you are serving" (Col. 3:23-24). Although in this instance Paul was specifically addressing Christian slaves, the principle has universal application.

The Book of Proverbs has a lot to say about both the virtue of work and the danger of indolence.

Diligent hands will rule, but laziness ends in slave labor (Proverbs 12:24).

All hard work brings a profit, but mere talk leads only to poverty (Proverbs 14:23).

One who is slack in his work is brother to one who destroys (Proverbs 18:9).

> **Do you see a man skilled in his work? He will serve before kings; he will not serve before obscure men** (Proverbs 22:29).

In Matthew 25:14-30 Jesus tells a parable that clearly reveals God's attitude toward our dying in seed form. A man going on a journey entrusts some of his money to three of his servants, giving five talents to one, two talents to another, and one talent to the third. The first two servants go out immediately and through diligent work and wise investments double their master's money. The third servant simply buries the talent he was given. (Sounds like a cemetery, doesn't it?) Upon the master's return, he praises and rewards the two faithful servants, saying, "Well done, good and faithful servant! You have been faithful with a few things; I will put you in charge of many things. Come and share your master's happiness!" (Matt. 25:21,23) For the third servant, however, he has only harsh words:

> **You wicked, lazy servant!...you should have put my money on deposit with the bankers, so that when I returned I would have received it back with interest. Take the talent from him and give it to the one who has the ten talents. For everyone who has will be given more, and he will have an abundance. Whoever does not have, even what he has will be taken from him. And throw that worthless servant outside, into the darkness, where there will be weeping and gnashing of teeth** (Matthew 25:26-30).

The servant who despised and ignored what his master gave him was judged as being both wicked and lazy. *Wicked* in Greek is *poneros*, which also means "malicious," "derelict," and "morally culpable" (Strong's G4190). In this context, **wickedness means dying with our glory. We are wicked if we do not bring forth our full selves, and do not reveal who we really are.** Life is all about dying empty. God wants us to pour out everything

Life is all about dying empty.

He has given us. If we fail to do so, especially when we have every opportunity, we are both wicked and lazy. Die empty of glory. Manifest your true self.

Don't Be Lazy

Laziness keeps our glory inside. People who don't want to do much never show their glory. If we want to maximize our glory and reveal our true selves, we must be prepared to work hard. *We cannot be lazy and reveal our glory.* People who maximize their glory are always tired. Tired, "poured-out" people are the ones who change the world.

Thomas Edison is credited with the invention of the first practical electric lightbulb. In the course of its development, he experimented with over 2,000 different filament materials before he found one that worked. What if he had given up after 1,999 attempts? The point I'm trying to make is that we'll never get anywhere by being lazy. How many times do we allow ourselves to fail at something before we quit, concluding that it obviously isn't God's will? Just because something is difficult and takes a lot of time and effort does not necessarily mean that it isn't right. **If something is *right*, it's *possible*.** If something is God's will, it's possible, no matter how difficult it appears. If something is God's will, it is worth every minute, every dollar, and every ounce of energy we expend on it.

Exposing our full glory is a lifelong process. In fact, it will cost us our lives. When our true glory comes out it will kill us. It was only when He died on the cross that Jesus fully revealed His glory as the only begotten Son of the Father and the Lamb of God who takes away the sin of the world. **Glory will consume us like a fire and drain us like poured-out wine. Our purpose in life is to get rid of our glory.** Life is about glory manifestation.

> **W**e cannot be lazy and reveal our glory.

Be Holy

We glorify God not only in our work but also in pursuing a lifestyle of personal holiness. Do you realize that the Bible never tells us to pray for holiness? It never tells us to fast for holiness, or to dress in a certain way or only eat certain foods. The Bible never tells us to *do* anything for holiness; instead, it simply says that we are to *be holy*.

> **I am the Lord who brought you up out of Egypt to be your God; therefore be holy, because I am holy** (Leviticus 11:45).

> **Consecrate yourselves and be holy, because I am the Lord your God. Keep My decrees and follow them. I am the Lord, who makes you holy** (Leviticus 20:7-8).

> **To the church of God in Corinth, to those sanctified in Christ Jesus and called to be holy...** (1 Corinthians 1:2a).

> **For He chose us in Him before the creation of the world to be holy and blameless in His sight** (Ephesians 1:4).

> **Make every effort to live in peace with all men and to be holy; without holiness no one will see the Lord** (Hebrews 12:14).

> **But just as He who called you is holy, so be holy in all you do; for it is written: "Be holy, because I am holy"** (1 Peter 1:15-16).

Whenever God commands us to "be" or "do" something, we can be confident that He has already built it into us. God will never demand anything of us that He will not equip us to accomplish. Whatever God demands, He supplies. He commands us to "be holy because I am holy." This means that since God is holy, and we came out of God, that we are holy as well. God made us in His image, and because He is holy, we who are made in His image are also holy.

As far as it relates to us, to be holy means to be set apart as God's special possession, or for God's special and exclusive use. To be holy means that we willingly place ourselves completely at God's disposal for Him to use as He pleases. Holiness also means to be perfect (complete) and spiritually pure.

A proper understanding of holiness and God's requirement that we "be holy" will affect both our attitude and our lifestyle. We cannot "be holy" and continue to think and live like the world. God has called us apart to Him, to live *in* the world as citizens of the Kingdom of Heaven. This calls for prayer, discipline, and careful attention on our part to ensure that everything we say and do, as well as the work we give our hand to every day, honors the Lord and brings glory to His name.

Sin impaired our ability to be holy, but did not destroy it. The Bible never says that man is "non-holy," which would be a reflection on our nature. Rather, it says that we are "unholy," which speaks to our will and to the choices we make. When Adam and Eve chose to disobey God in the Garden of Eden, they did not become "non-holy"; they became "unholy." Sin is a *choice*. Possessed of the nature of God Himself, Adam and Eve *chose* to disregard it. Ever since, sin has caused us to make unholy choices and live in an unholy manner.

Jesus Christ came to remove sin's impediment to our being holy. He took our sins with Him to the cross, removing them from us and fully restoring our ability to be holy as God is holy. The Holy Spirit who indwells us as believers is the agent of our holiness, promoting it and building it in our lives as we willingly yield to His control.

> **W**e cannot "be holy" and continue to think and live like the world.

It doesn't matter where you are living right now, what your circumstances are, or what you are doing. As long as you are not openly living in sin, God can take you from where you are to where He wants you to be. It all depends on your attitude, the condition of your heart, and the choices you make. Your environment does not have to determine your atmosphere.

I was born in Bains Town, in the Bahamas, which was generally a low-income area. In that environment it was easy to go either one way or the other. There were many influences there that could have dragged me down. Instead, I decided to create my own atmosphere. I determined not to let my environment prevent me from fulfilling my dreams. Through His grace, God made it possible. What I'm trying to say is that where we live is not necessarily where we have to exist. With God's help we can create our own environment, an atmosphere of faith, confidence, praise, worship, and hope.

The glory of "becoming" is discovering what we were born to do, putting our hand diligently to that work for the glory of God, and growing in a lifestyle of personal holiness so that everyone we meet will experience the presence of God and come to understand His eternal purpose for them in Christ.

❖ PRINCIPLES ❖

1. God created us to find satisfaction in our work within the framework of a personal love relationship with Him through Christ.

2. There is no competition when it comes to glory. Our roles may all be different, but our purpose is the same: to glorify God.

3. God does not want us to die in seed form.

4. Glorifying God means releasing our full potential. We do this in two ways: by the work we do every day and by pursuing a life of personal holiness.

5. Life is all about dying empty.

6. We cannot be lazy and reveal our glory.

7. Just because something is difficult and takes a lot of time and effort does not necessarily mean that it isn't right. If something is *right*, it's *possible*.

8. Glory will consume us like a fire and drain us like poured-out wine. Our purpose in life is to get rid of our glory. Life is about glory manifestation.

9. God will never demand anything of us that He will not equip us to accomplish.

10. We cannot "be holy" and continue to think and live like the world.

11. Your environment does not have to determine your atmosphere.

12. The glory of "becoming" is discovering what we were born to do, putting our hand diligently to that work

for the glory of God, and growing in a lifestyle of personal holiness so that everyone we meet will experience the presence of God and come to understand His eternal purpose for them in Christ.

Chapter Five

The Presence and the Glory

**If we want to see the glory of God
we must live in the presence of God.**

Every creature on earth lives at the bottom of a great ocean. It surrounds us wherever we go and provides the environment in which we live and breathe. Remove us from this ocean unprepared and we will die in a matter of seconds. It protects us from the ravages of solar and cosmic radiation and from being pelted to death by the thousands of meteors and micrometeorites that cross our path every year.

Of course, the "ocean" I am referring to is the earth's atmosphere. All land-based plants and animals (as well as seagoing mammals such as whales and dolphins) are perfectly adapted to life in an ocean of air. Our lives depend on it. God prepared the perfect physical environment, then placed in it the creatures for which He had designed it.

❖ The Glory of Living

Until recent years, when concerns over pollution, ozone depletion, greenhouse gases, and general air quality have raised our ecological awareness, human beings pretty much took the earth's environment for granted. We lived our daily lives without giving much thought to the air we breathed (unless for some reason we suddenly had trouble breathing—then it got our attention!).

There is another environment that is critical to human life. Its absence is just as deadly but not as immediately noticeable as a loss of air. Just as we cannot survive without air, we cannot function without the presence of God. Without God's presence we cannot fully display our glory. Mankind lost the presence of God at the Fall, but most of us act as though we don't even miss it.

One of the problems across much of the religious world today is that so many live as if there is no such thing as glory. Countless believers spend their days working, playing, going to church, raising families, attending school, and doing all the other ordinary things of life with no real sense of the presence of God and seeing little evidence of His glory. They have become so accustomed to humdrum, mundane, and powerless lives that they have accepted blandness and mediocrity as the norm. No longer do they expect to witness any great movement of God or experience any fresh outpouring of the Spirit in their own hearts. Focused as they are on the daily grind, they can't even see the quiet evidence of God at work right around them.

Does this describe your life? Do you find yourself working hard day after day, yet nothing seems to be happening? Do you involve yourself in religious activities and do all the right religious stuff and still find that your life is dull and flat? Are you starved for the presence and glory of God and longing for signs of His power in your life?

Despite the experiences of so many, it is not normal for believers to go through life with no sense of God's presence or power. Walking with God under the covering shelter of His presence should be our day-by-day, moment-by-moment experience. When it is not, something is wrong. An incident in the life of the nation of Israel has given us a word that defines the condition of God's people living apart from His presence, and therefore outside of His will: *Ichabod.*

"The Glory Has Departed"

In the fourth chapter of the Book of First Samuel the Israelites suffer a massive defeat at the hands of the Philistines (see 1 Sam. 4:1-11). The battle occurred in two stages. During the first encounter, the Hebrews lost four thousand soldiers. Analyzing this setback, the Israelite leaders concluded that their defeat was due to the fact that they did not have the ark of the covenant with them in battle.

The ark of the covenant was the gold-covered wooden box that God had commanded Moses to make and which contained the stone tablets of the Ten Commandments. On top of the ark was the golden "mercy seat" with its two golden cherubim facing each other. It was between these cherubim that the presence of God resided. To the Israelites, the ark of the covenant represented the very real presence of God in their midst.

> **So the people sent men to Shiloh, and they brought back the ark of the covenant of the Lord Almighty, who is enthroned between the cherubim. And Eli's two sons, Hophni and Phinehas, were there with the ark of the covenant of God** (1 Samuel 4:4).

Shiloh was the semi-permanent location of the tabernacle, where the ark was kept in the Holy of Holies. As priests, Eli's sons Hophni and Phinehas accompanied the ark to the Israelites' battle camp. By law only priests and Levites could transport or handle the ark. Eli was a true priest and servant of God, but had failed to pass this legacy on to his sons. Corrupt and immoral, Hophni and Phinehas were unfit to be priests. In fact, the Scripture plainly states, "Eli's sons were wicked men; they had no regard for the Lord" (1 Sam. 2:12). Ungodly priests in charge of the ark was one indication of the problem in the Hebrew camp.

The Israelites greeted the ark's arrival with great excitement and rejoicing. *God* was with them; *now* they would be victorious! When the Philistines learned that the ark had arrived, fear swept their ranks. They had heard of the great deeds of power and deliverance that the God of the Hebrews had performed. Preparing for the worst, the Philistines geared up to fight for all they were worth, deciding that it was better to die in battle than to serve as slaves to the Israelites (see 1 Sam. 4:6-9).

As it turned out, however, Israel fared worse in the second encounter than in the first.

So the Philistines fought, and the Israelites were defeated and every man fled to his tent. The slaughter was very great; Israel lost thirty thousand foot soldiers. The ark of God was captured, and Eli's two sons, Hophni and Phinehas, died (1 Samuel 4:10-11).

Back in Shiloh, when Eli heard that the ark had been captured and both his sons killed, he fell backward off his chair, broke his neck, and died. The deaths of Eli and his sons fulfilled a prophecy the Lord had given to young Samuel that He would judge the house of Eli both for the wickedness of his sons as well as for Eli's failure to restrain them (see 1 Sam. 3:11-14).

At the same time, Eli's daughter-in-law, the wife of his son Phinehas, was pregnant and near delivery. The news of the ark's capture and the deaths of Eli and Phinehas sent her into labor. She gave birth to a son, but the travail of delivery killed her. With her dying breath she exclaimed her grief:

She named the boy Ichabod, saying, "The glory has departed from Israel"—because of the capture of the ark of God and the deaths of her father-in-law and her husband.

She said, "The glory has departed from Israel, for the ark of God has been captured" (1 Samuel 4:21-22).

The name *Ichabod* literally means "no glory." It is a combination of the word *kabod* (glory) with the prefix *iy*, which means "not" (Strong's H336, H350, H3519). When the ark of God departed, the presence of God departed, and when the presence of God departed, the glory of God departed.

In reality, the loss of the ark was a visual fulfillment of what had already happened spiritually in Israel. Defeat came not because the *ark* was absent, but because the *presence of God* was absent. The Israelites had already turned away from God and were not following or obeying Him. By presuming upon God they had ensured their own defeat. Taking the ark into battle demonstrated that they had substituted a *symbol* of God's presence for the *reality* of His presence. They treated the ark as if it were a talisman that would magically protect them. Because of their presumptuous pride, God allowed the ark to be captured. The covering presence and protection of God had *already* departed and they didn't even know it!

Pursuing God's Presence to Expose God's Glory

No one can fully fulfill God's purpose for them without His presence. The Israelites couldn't and neither can we. Without the energizing power of God we cannot maximize our full potential or bring out the ultimate glory hidden within us. In order to expose God's glory in us we must pursue His manifest presence around us. God's presence paves the way for His glory. We cannot see God's glory without His presence.

The presence of God is when God allows us to "pre-sense" Him before He shows up and fully manifests Himself. We get a "sense" of God before He reveals His full glory. That is why it is so important to praise God whenever we come together. Praise attracts God's presence. We praise God so that we can glorify Him. God's presence is a prerequisite for relationship with Him. Abel, the second son of Adam and Eve, was the first to understand the importance of God's presence. He offered an acceptable sacrifice to the Lord because he was hungry for God's presence, and his brother Cain killed him because of it. The presence of God is critical for seeing His glory.

Today we face the same choice that Cain, Abel, and the Israelites faced. As long as the Israelites were faithful to God, obeyed Him, and were hungry for His continuing presence with them, they experienced peace, victory, and prosperity, and fulfilled God's purpose for them as a nation. Their glory shone forth as they followed the destiny God had set for them. When they disobeyed and turned away from God, they faced His judgment. God withdrew His presence and His glory departed with it. We need to ask ourselves which condition we want to characterize our lives: *kabod* or *ichabod*, "glory" or "no glory."

Many of us today live in a state of *ichabod*, seeing no evidence of God's glory and sensing little of His presence. This may be due to our disobedience or to the presence of unconfessed sin in our lives. It may be due to spiritual laziness and lack of discipline: We simply can't be bothered with the deeper things of the Spirit. It may be that we simply are not hungry for God; we've decided that things are okay the way they are and have convinced ourselves that we are content with the status quo.

Whatever the reason, our situation won't change until we decide to do something about it. God wants more for us than a mundane spiritual life. He wants to reveal His glory in us and help us reach our full potential, but He will not force it on us. God responds to us in proportion to the hunger of our hearts. As long as we are satisfied the way we are, God will allow us to stay that way. He may nudge us or prod us to try to awaken in us a greater desire for Him, but the final decision is ours.

That's why exposing God's glory in us is hard work. It's not enough simply to say, "I glorify God"; we must demonstrate in our lives and in our daily work the evidence of God's grace and mercy abounding toward us and reaching out to others. Our lives must be seasoned with grace, humility, love, and discipline. However, these characteristics will not come automatically; we must cultivate them patiently, carefully, and prayerfully in the Holy Spirit.

> *I*n order to expose God's glory in us we must pursue His manifest presence around us.

We cannot glorify God without His presence, and we will not experience His presence unless we are hungry for Him. If we want the glory of God to come out in our lives, we must pursue His presence. When God's presence comes, He will reveal His glory.

God's Presence Versus God's Glory

As I mentioned in Chapter Two, it is important to understand the difference between the presence of God and the glory of God. Contrary to the impression of many Christians, God's presence and God's glory are not necessarily one and the same. The presence of God is the active manifestation of God that fills the environment in which creation exists and lives, while glory is the open display of His attributes and character. It is often easy to confuse the two. God's presence is all-pervasive but invisible. His glory, on the other hand, is tangible and observable. Although at times it may be hidden, it is never invisible.

When we talk about the presence of God, we also need to distinguish between His *omnipresence* and His *manifest presence*. God's omnipresence simply means that He is everywhere. The Bible reveals this about God even though it never plainly states it. For example, David, the shepherd-king of Israel, writes:

> **Where can I go from Your Spirit? Where can I flee from Your presence? If I go up to the heavens, You are there; if I make my bed in the depths, You are there. If I rise on the wings of the dawn, if I settle on the far side of the sea, even there Your hand will guide me, Your right hand will hold me fast. If I say, "Surely the darkness will hide me and the light become night around me," even the darkness will not be dark to You; the night will shine like the day, for darkness is as light to You** (Psalm 139:7-12).

God's presence is everywhere in the context of His creation. This is different from both animism, which attributes conscious life to all elements in nature, both animate and inanimate, and pantheism, which equates God with the forces and laws of the universe. Animists believe that God *inhabits* all things, while pantheists believe that God *is* all things. This is not what the Bible teaches. The creature *is not* the Creator! The omnipresent God of the Bible *created* nature and all its elements. He *created* the forces and laws which govern the universe. God is above and separate from His creation, yet He surrounds it and infuses it with His life. As David says, we cannot flee from God's presence or go away from His Spirit. God is omnipresent because He is God and because, no matter how great the created universe appears to our finite minds, He is greater still, infinitely greater.

The *manifest* presence of God is when God takes the initiative to make Himself known to us in a specific and focused way that goes beyond His general omnipresence. Although not exact, one way to understand this is to say that we know God's omnipresence by *faith* and His manifest presence by *experience*. God's omnipresence is evident in creation to any who are willing to believe, but none of us can experience God's manifest presence unless He chooses to reveal Himself.

Moses spent 40 years herding sheep in the deserts of Midian surrounded by the omnipresence of God, yet he knew nothing of the manifest presence of God until the day God spoke to him from the midst of a burning bush. In the face of this intense and focused encounter with a holy God, Moses took off his shoes and fell on his face in fear and reverence. As a result, Moses came to know God in a deeply personal way.

God does not hide from us. He has promised in His Word that all who seek Him will find Him. Once again, it goes back to the issue of the hunger of our hearts. God initiates but He never coerces. **God will not enter where He is not invited, but He will freely reveal Himself to those who open their hearts to Him.**

The glory of God is the open manifestation of His attributes and His nature, the exposure of His character and His power. God's glory is when He literally lets us see Him at work. A good example of the relationship between God's presence and His glory is the experience of the nation of Israel. When Moses led the Israelites out of Egypt, God revealed Himself to them in progressively specific ways. The Israelites experienced God's presence when He answered their cries and prayers for deliverance. They experienced His manifest presence when He revealed Himself in a pillar of smoke by day and a pillar of fire by night. They experienced God's glory when He parted the Red Sea. Another way to describe this relationship is to say that when we experience God's omnipresence we know His existence, when we experience God's manifest presence we know His holiness, and when we experience God's glory we know His power.

When we experience God's omnipresence we know His existence, when we experience God's manifest presence we know His holiness, and when we experience God's glory we know His power.

Five Keys to Releasing the Glory of God

What can we do to make sure that the word *ichabod*—"no glory"—is not written across the pages of our lives? How can we see the glory of God released in us? Here are five important keys to remember. I have touched on some of them already.

1. *The glory of God needs the presence of God in order to be manifested.* Just as a seed needs the soil to bring forth the tree that's trapped inside, so we need the presence of God to bring forth the person—our true self—that He created us to become. No matter how high our goals or how lofty our dreams, they will never come to pass until we create the right atmosphere in the presence of God.

2. *The presence of God is conducive to the glory of God.* In other words, the presence is the conduit through which the glory comes. Just as electricity needs a conductive substance in order for current to flow through a circuit, so God's glory needs a conductor in order to flow into and out of our lives. That conductor is the presence of God. God's presence provides the conducive or proper environment for us to bring forth the glory that's trapped inside of us.

3. *Man was created to live and function in the presence of God.* Outside God's presence we malfunction. If we are outside of God's presence, we cannot bring forth the glory that's on the inside. When God created us in His image, with His likeness and possessed of His spiritual characteristics, He created us to function like Him. Sin took us out of God's covering presence, and made us unholy. God knows that we cannot function properly without His presence, and He will do whatever is necessary to restore us. That's why Jesus came, to cleanse us from sin with His blood, change our

unholiness to holiness, our unrighteousness to righteousness, and bring us back into the conducive environment of God's presence so the glory in us can come out.

4.   *Praise is the ideal environment for man and creation.* If the presence of God is the necessary and conducive environment for the glory to come out, and if we were created to function in God's presence, then praise is the ideal environment for us. Why? Because *praise attracts the presence.* **We don't praise God to glorify Him but to get His presence in our midst.** Praise is something we can do anytime, anywhere: in the car or on the bus, in the bathroom or in the bedroom, while standing over a stove cooking dinner or sitting in front of a computer screen at work, alone or with a group. Psalm 34:1 (KJV) says, "I will bless the Lord at all times: His praise shall continually be in my mouth." He has given each one of us our own private praise ministry. God wants us to praise Him continually because He wants us in His presence continually. Praise makes it possible. Praise attracts the presence of God, maintains the presence of God, and is a prerequisite for the presence of God. When we praise God with our lips and our hearts, He shows His approval and acceptance by manifesting His presence in our midst. That is when worship—*true* worship—takes place.

5.   *The presence of God releases the glory of God.* When all these things are in place, when all the keys are in order, God will manifest His presence and release His glory. This is not a "formula" by which we can force God to dance to our tune. God is sovereign; He cannot be manipulated. The critical factor is the attitude of our spirit. God responds eagerly and willingly to the

hunger, the heart cries and the praise of people who approach Him in humility, repentance, and love. The glory of God comes out only in the presence of God, and the presence of God arrives only in the midst of our praise. Psalm 22:3 (KJV) says, "But Thou art holy, O Thou that inhabitest the praises of Israel." God's presence allows us to function and bring forth His glory. Once we truly understand that we need God's presence in order to become all we were born to be, then His presence will become more important to us than anything else in the world, and we will do whatever is necessary to get it.

The Pitcher and the Glass

What then are the characteristics of a *kabod* lifestyle, one that is filled and spilling over with the glory of God? Psalm 8:5 says that God made man a little lower than Himself and crowned us with glory and honor. In other words, He is God and we are "gods," in the sense that we are patterned after His likeness. He is the pitcher, we are the glasses. God pours out some of Himself into us and wants to keep pouring until we overflow. He wants to bring out His glory in us in order to bless others. He wants us to bring out our glory, to "let [our] light shine before men, that they may see [our] good deeds and praise [our] Father in heaven" (Matt. 5:16).

> **W**hen we "pour out" our lives to others in Jesus' name they will drink of us but will taste Him.

God's purpose and desire is that all people everywhere have the opportunity to taste His living water. Psalm 34:8 says, "Taste and see that the Lord is good; blessed is the man who takes refuge in Him." How does one "taste" God? By talking to someone who has Him on display. By meeting someone who expresses in his life the glory, the attributes, and the character of God. That's how you get to know what God is like.

Too often when people try to drink they can't taste God because the water in our glass is polluted by our fleshly living and carnal minds. That's why it is so important for us to be godly people. We are to be holy because God is holy. As the pitcher is, so the glass should be. A person who is living the *kabod* life lives to share the water of God with other thirsty people. "Taste and see that the Lord is good" means "God is the pitcher, I am the glass. If you want to taste Him, come drink some of my life." The best way for people to know God is to meet us. When we "pour out" our lives to others in Jesus' name they will drink of us but will taste Him. The purpose for your life is to fill the earth with the glory of your life.

❖ PRINCIPLES ❖

1. Walking with God under the covering shelter of His presence should be our day-by-day, moment-by-moment experience.

2. In order to expose God's glory in us we must pursue His manifest presence around us.

3. When we experience God's omnipresence we know His existence; when we experience God's manifest presence we know His holiness; and when we experience God's glory we know His power.

4. The glory of God needs the presence of God in order to be manifested.

5. The presence of God is conducive to the glory of God.

6. Man was created to live and function in the presence of God.

7. Praise is the ideal environment for man and creation.

8. Praise attracts the presence of God, maintains the presence of God, and is a prerequisite for the presence of God.

9. When we praise God with our lips and our hearts, He shows His approval and acceptance by manifesting His presence in our midst. That is when worship—*true* worship—takes place.

10. The presence of God releases the glory of God.

11. When we "pour out" our lives to others in Jesus' name they will drink of us but will taste Him.

Chapter Six

Restoring the Environment of Glory

Our praise recreates the spiritual environment of Eden and attracts God's presence.

In the beginning, after God had created the world and all its vast array of life, and "had planted a garden in the east, in Eden" (Gen. 2:8), He placed Adam there "to work it and take care of it" (Gen. 2:15). Later, God fashioned Eve from part of Adam's side and presented her to him as his mate and companion. Adam and Eve found that Eden was the perfect environment in which to thrive and prosper because it was the place where the presence of God surrounded them. It was only as they remained in God's presence that they could realize their full potential and become all that they were created to be. **The presence of God is the ideal environment for man's glory.**

❖ The Glory of Living

God's original desire and design was for Adam and Eve and their descendants to reproduce "Eden" throughout the earth as they obeyed God's command to "be fruitful and increase in number; fill the earth and subdue it" (Gen. 1:28b). Mankind did indeed fill the earth and subdued it to a large degree, but sin separated us from God and removed us from God's presence. As a result, we were cut off from Eden and the earth was filled with the consequences of our sin: war, hatred, violence, selfishness, suffering, and despair. Those are characteristics of a world outside the covering presence of God.

Today we still struggle daily with those consequences, even as believers. There is a restlessness in us, although we may not always recognize its source. Our hearts and our spirits yearn and long to return to Eden, to that bright, vibrant, and vital relationship with God that is characterized by His continual presence in our lives. The mundane and worldly circumstances that surround us on a daily basis resist our efforts to walk with God. Discouragement and negativity abound everywhere we look. We have no trouble at all finding dead-end people who would like nothing better than for us to join them in their mediocrity. Misery loves company. People whose lives are going nowhere fear and resent those who are determined to rise above their circumstances.

Don't forget that our circumstances do not have to dictate our environment. God has enabled us, in a sense, to re-create Eden in our lives. Through the blood of Christ and the indwelling Holy Spirit we can create our *own* environment that draws the presence of God near. That environment is the atmosphere of *praise.* Psalm 22:3 says that God inhabits the praises of His people, so when God's people praise Him, He draws near and worship results. God has given each of us a praise ministry with a worship "team" that is never any farther away than an inch below our nose: our lips, mouth, and tongue.

God does not need either our praise or our worship—He is God no matter what we do or don't do—but *we* need His presence.

God's presence comes through our praise. If we desire to live a *kabod* lifestyle, we must learn to cultivate a continual environment of praise. Hebrews 13:15 says, "Through Jesus, therefore, let us continually offer to God a sacrifice of praise—the fruit of lips that confess His name." Praise is a sacrificial offering to God, the spiritual "firstfruits" of our lips.

One way to look at praise is to think of it as "bragging" on God. When we praise the Lord, we are telling Him all the good and wonderful things about Himself. Praise is bragging on God's nature, attributes, and character; it is agreeing with God concerning what He has already told us about Himself.

When we praise God, His presence comes near, and in His presence all our true glory can be released. We cannot create this environment of praise completely on our own. That's why Christ gave us His Spirit. Jesus said, "I am the vine; you are the branches. If a man remains in Me and I in him, he will bear much fruit; apart from Me you can do nothing" (Jn. 15:5). In our own strength we can do nothing. When we abide in Christ and remain joined to Him as the branch is joined to the vine, we can do anything He wants us to do. Praise is something we can do anytime, anywhere. As we learn to exercise our personal praise ministry, **we can create "islands of Eden" around us wherever we go.**

There is an inseparable link between our praise and the manifest presence of God. In the last chapter I briefly stated some principles regarding this relationship, but they are so important that I want to elaborate on them.

Praise Attracts the Presence of God

One thing I want to make crystal clear is the importance of the presence of God. It is one thing to know of God's omnipresence, but quite another to experience the reality of His personal presence on a continuing day-to-day basis. Before anything else, we *need* the presence of God. Everything else in life depends on God's presence.

Praise attracts the presence of God. True praise is an exercise, a discipline that flows from a pure heart and a humble spirit. When we "brag" about God we are acknowledging His sovereignty and Lordship as well as our own dependence on Him. That spirit of humility is just what God is looking for in us. Consider these words from James:

> **Submit yourselves, then, to God. Resist the devil, and he will flee from you. Come near to God and He will come near to you. Wash your hands, you sinners, and purify your hearts, you double-minded. Grieve, mourn and wail. Change your laughter to mourning and your joy to gloom. Humble yourselves before the Lord, and He will lift you up** (James 4:7-10).

These verses are filled with the language of humility and repentance. The words *submit, come near,* and *humble yourselves* all relate to humility, while *wash your hands, purify your hearts, grieve, mourn and wail, mourning,* and *gloom* deal with repentance. If we approach God with a humble spirit He will do two things: When we "come near to God," He will "come near" to us; and when we "humble" ourselves before Him, He will lift us up.

One of the ways we come near to God is through praise because praise establishes an environment in which God is pleased to dwell. When we lift up praise we are agreeing with God concerning Himself, which is a complete reversal of what Adam and Eve did in the Garden of Eden. Remember what satan said when he tempted Eve: "Did God really say, 'You must not eat from any tree in the garden'?" (Gen. 3:1b) With that question satan was implying, "I disagree with God, and I want you to disagree with Him, too." Taken in by satan's deception, Eve decided she disagreed with God also, and even passed her disagreement on to her husband. Adam and Eve may have called it "disagreement," but God called it sin.

Sin is rebellion against the known, revealed will of God. It is disagreement with what God says. Sin is what got Adam and Eve kicked out of Eden and removed from God's covering presence. It also broke their relationship with God, a breach that was inherited by all their descendants. For everyone who trusts Him in faith, the blood of Christ cleanses us from sin and restores our broken relationship with God. The praise of our lips, whether alone or as a congregation of believers, re-creates the spiritual environment of Eden, and attracts God's presence. Praise is one way we "come near to God," and when we do, He comes near to us.

> **P**raise establishes an environment in which God is pleased to dwell.

Praise reverses the sin of the Garden of Eden because we are now agreeing with God concerning Himself and His words. When we agree with God in humility and faith, He draws near. When we say, "Oh Lord, You're beautiful," He says, "I agree with that. I'm coming closer." We say, "Oh Lord, You're mighty," and He says, "Finally, You agree with Me! I'm coming closer." **Praise is always positive. There is no such thing as negative praise. We cannot "praise" in disagreement; that's nothing more than criticism.**

Sin is rebellion against God, but praise reflects our relationship with God. We can praise God *because* we have a relationship with Him through Christ. When we praise God we draw near to Him, agree with what He has said about His nature, attributes, and character, and create an environment conducive to His presence. As a result, He draws near to us. **Praise attracts God's presence.**

Praise Maintains the Presence of God

If praise is necessary to attract God's presence, then it is also necessary to maintain His presence. The Bible depicts God on His throne in Heaven surrounded by an atmosphere of unceasing praise.

> **In the year that King Uzziah died, I saw the Lord seated on a throne, high and exalted, and the train of His robe filled the temple. Above Him were seraphs, each with six wings: With two wings they covered their faces, with two they covered their feet, and with two they were flying. And they were calling to one another: "Holy, holy, holy is the Lord Almighty; the whole earth is full of His glory." At the sound of their voices the doorposts and thresholds shook and the temple was filled with smoke** (Isaiah 6:1-4).

In the Book of Revelation, John describes God as seated on a throne guarded by four angelic beings who praise Him continually:

> **Each of the four living creatures had six wings and was covered with eyes all around, even under his wings. Day and night they never stop saying: "Holy, holy, holy is the Lord God Almighty, who was, and is, and is to come"** (Revelation 4:8).

Taking their cue from the four angels, the 24 elders surrounding the throne also lift up their praise:

> **"You are worthy, our Lord and God, to receive glory and honor and power, for You created all things, and by Your will they were created and have their being"** (Revelation 4:11).

The inhabitants of Heaven praise God with undiluted and undivided devotion. Likewise for us, praise that not only attracts but also maintains God's presence must be offered from pure hearts that are wholly devoted to Him. Half-hearted praise won't cut it. We are to praise God at *all* times, even when we don't feel like it. The wonderful thing about praise is that when we start doing it even though we're not in the mood, before long the very act of praise will *put* us in the mood. Although our feelings and moods change, the position of our heart should not, and it is our heart that God looks at. David's heart was always positioned toward God, even when his feelings or moods led him into sin. A humble heart praises God; a proud heart does not. True praise comes only from a humble heart that is focused on God.

Halfhearted or insincere praise does not honor God, and He will not then honor us with His presence. God is holy and will not pretend that we are honoring Him when we really are not. This was one of the great repeated sins of the nation of Israel. Praise and worship degenerated into meaningless and hypocritical ritual where the so-called "praise" on their lips was completely detached from the attitude in their hearts.

> **T**rue praise comes only from a humble heart that is focused on God.

> **The Lord says: "These people come near to Me with their mouth and honor Me with their lips, but their hearts are far from Me. Their worship of Me is made up only of rules taught by men"** (Isaiah 29:13).

Jesus quoted this same verse when He challenged the Pharisees over their practice of placing the traditions of men above the laws of God (see Matt. 15:1-9).

The full blessings of the presence of God are reserved for those who come to Him and praise Him with a whole heart. David the psalmist described that kind of people.

> **Who may ascend the hill of the Lord? Who may stand in His holy place? He who has clean hands and a pure heart, who does not lift up his soul to an idol or swear by what is false. He will receive blessing from the Lord and vindication from God his Savior. Such is the generation of those who seek Him, who seek Your face, O God of Jacob** (Psalm 24:3-6).

Whenever we praise the Lord with our lips but our heart is not in it, He won't pretend it is real, even if we do. That's why it is so important for us to fully engage both our minds and our hearts in our praise. Wholehearted praise maintains God's presence.

Praise Is a Prerequisite for the Presence of God

Throughout the Bible we find examples of God's presence being ushered in by the praises of His people. The pattern is common enough for us to conclude that, generally speaking, praise is a prerequisite for the presence of God. This is not absolute, of course, because God is sovereign, accountable to no one except Himself, and works in whatever way suits His purpose. For example, the Bible does not tell us whether or not Abram was praising God before God spoke to him and promised to grow a nation from his descendants (see Gen. 12:1-3). Likewise, we do not know if Moses was engaged in praise prior to his encounter with God's presence in the burning bush (see Ex. 3).

In general, however, God does not visit His people with His presence without their first lifting up His praise. **We do not invite God's presence in, or even pray His presence in, as much as we** *praise* **His presence into a place.** This is a principle by which God Himself has chosen to work. Several examples from the Scriptures will illustrate this.

When Joshua was preparing to lead the Israelites to conquer the walled city of Jericho, God gave him special instructions.

> **Then the Lord said to Joshua, "See, I have delivered Jericho into your hands, along with its king and its fighting men. March around the city once with all the armed men. Do this for six days. Have seven priests carry trumpets of rams' horns in front of the ark. On the seventh day, march around the city seven times, with the priests blowing the trumpets. When you hear them sound a long blast on the trumpets, have all the people give a loud shout; then the wall of the city will collapse and the people will go up, every man straight in."...When the trumpets sounded, the**

people shouted, and at the sound of the trumpet, when the people gave a loud shout, the wall collapsed; so every man charged straight in, and they took the city (Joshua 6:2-5;20).

Although this passage does not specifically state that the Israelites were praising God, the Hebrew word *rua*, which is here translated "shout" and "shouted," is the same word used in Psalm 100:1 and Psalm 95:1 and translated "shout joyfully," or "make a joyful noise." Other meanings include "battle cry," "shout of triumph," and "sound an alarm." *Rua* was "used to denote any shout of joy or praise. In public worship it would denote praise of the most animated kind."[1] The priests blew the trumpets; the people raised a great shout of joy, triumph, and praise; God's presence and power came down; and the walls of Jericho fell flat. When the praise went up the presence came down.

On the Day of Pentecost, 120 believers were gathered together in an upper room in Jerusalem when the presence of God came down and they were all "filled with the Holy Spirit and began to speak in other tongues as the Spirit enabled them" (Acts 2:4). This was in fulfillment of Jesus' promises to them:

And I will ask the Father, and He will give you another Counselor to be with you forever—the Spirit of truth (John 14:16-17a).

But you will receive power when the Holy Spirit comes on you; and you will be My witnesses in Jerusalem, and in all Judea and Samaria, and to the ends of the earth (Acts 1:8).

I am going to send you what My Father has promised; but stay in the city until you have been clothed with power from on high (Luke 24:49).

---

1.   Albert Barnes, *Barnes' Notes on the Old Testament* (Cedar Rapids, IA: Parsons Technology, Inc., Electronic Edition STEP Files, 1999), notes on Ps. 95:1.

Jesus gave the last two of these promises on the day He ascended to Heaven; the Spirit came ten days later. The disciples were not idle during that time, however. They spent those days preparing for His coming by creating an environment of praise:

When He had led them out to the vicinity of Bethany, He lifted up His hands and blessed them. While He was blessing them, He left them and was taken up into heaven. Then they worshiped Him and returned to Jerusalem with great joy. And they stayed continually at the temple, praising God (Luke 24:50-53).

Once, in the city of Philippi, Paul and Silas found themselves thrown into jail on trumped-up charges by the owners of a slave girl who had made her masters a lot of money fortune-telling until Paul cast the demon out of her. Stripped, severely beaten, and with their feet locked in stocks, the two missionaries were not in a conducive environment for God's presence. So they decided to create their own.

About midnight Paul and Silas were praying and singing hymns to God, and the other prisoners were listening to them. Suddenly there was such a violent earthquake that the foundations of the prison were shaken. At once all the prison doors flew open, and everybody's chains came loose (Acts 16:25-26).

The basic definition of the word *hymn* is "a song of praise to God." Paul and Silas were singing praise songs to the Lord when His presence came down and shook the foundations of the prison. In Greek the word translated "singing hymns" is *humneo,* a verb which also specifically means "praise" and "singing hymns *of praise.*" In fact, other Bible versions are more specific: Paul and Silas "sang praises unto God" (KJV); they were "singing hymns of praise to God" (NAS).

Clearly, praise was present in the prison before the presence came down. Through praise, Paul and Silas turned their prison into an "Eden" of God's presence. As a result, that same night the jailer and his entire family were saved. Praise is a prerequisite for God's presence.

Worship Results When God Accepts Our Praise and Manifests His Presence

There is a difference between praise and worship. Praise is both a precursor to and a part of worship, but the two are not the same. Praise is something we do, while worship is something God releases. We initiate praise; it comes from within our hearts. As we perfect or mature our praise, as we come into one accord with one another, and as our spirit aligns with God's Spirit, He releases His presence into our midst. That mingling of God's presence with our praise is called worship.

Worship, then, begins with us as we lift up our praise, but it ends with God as He releases His presence among us. True worship requires both. We can praise the Lord until we're blue in the face, sing all sorts of songs, even work up a hot and holy sweat by our efforts, but if God's presence does not come down, we have not worshiped. On the other hand, God cannot release His presence without worshipers to receive Him. If it is true that we seek God's presence, it is equally true that He seeks worshipers. Jesus said to the Samaritan woman at the well, "Yet a time is coming and has now come when the true worshipers will worship the Father in spirit and truth, for they are the kind of worshipers the Father seeks. God is spirit, and His worshipers must worship in spirit and in truth" (Jn. 4:23-24).

To "worship in spirit and truth" has the idea of mingling with God spirit to Spirit with our hearts attuned to His heart and our thoughts attuned to His thoughts. In fact, the Greek word for "worship," *proskuneo*, literally means "to kiss, like a dog licking his master's hand; to prostrate oneself in homage" (Strong's G4352). It is a compound word, derived from *pros*, meaning "by the side of, near to, or toward" (Strong's G4314), and *kuneo*, which means "to kiss."[2] According to Strong's, the word is probably derived also from *kuon*, which means "dog" (Strong's G4352, G2965). Worship, then, means "to kiss the hand toward," as in showing honor and obeisance to royalty. It is also a word suggestive of intimate contact, of being in the very presence of someone of great importance, and of a companion who is always at his master's side. Anyway you look at it, worship involves intimacy.

Worship takes place when God dwells in our praise and begins to mingle with us. In a sense, we get close enough to God to kiss Him. Ultimately, worship depends not on us, but on God. God wants nothing more than to mingle with us in unbroken and unhindered fellowship, but it is not automatic. He requires that we desire Him and seek Him with all our heart, but He also promises that when we do that, we will find Him.

> **You will seek Me and find Me when you seek Me with all your heart** (Jeremiah 29:13).

> **Ask and it will be given to you; seek and you will find; knock and the door will be opened to you. For everyone who asks receives; he who seeks finds; and to him who knocks, the door will be opened** (Matthew 7:7-8).

> **Seek the Lord while He may be found; call on Him while He is near. Let the wicked forsake his way and the evil man his thoughts. Let him turn to the Lord, and He will have mercy on him, and to our God, for He will freely pardon** (Isaiah 55:6-7).

This is why pure-hearted, wholehearted praise is so important. **Without praise there is no presence, and without presence there is no worship**. Tragically, this is exactly what happens week after week after week in thousands of churches all over the world. Many

---

2. W.E. Vine, et al., *Vine's Complete Expository Dictionary of Old and New Testament Words* (Nashville, TN: Thomas Nelson Publishers, 1985), New Testament section, p. 686, "worshiping."

churches have not experienced genuine worship in years. They follow the same format every week, sing the same hymns or praise and worship songs the same way all the time, hear the same kinds of powerless prayers and the same insipid sermons every week, and the spirit is as dead as a doornail because their heart is no longer in it. This is true not only in many "mainline" churches, but in many evangelical and Pentecostal/charismatic churches as well.

God doesn't want it to be this way. He wants to bless us with His presence. The critical issue is the condition of our heart. If we seek God with a humble, hungry, and whole heart, lifting up sincere, heartfelt praise, He will respond by drawing us into His presence. In this way, we can recreate "Eden" through praise.

This whole matter of praise and worship also relates to exposing our hidden glory. When we praise God, He sends His presence, and His presence releases the glory. When we live in "Eden" our glory will come out. That's the way God designed things from the beginning. What this means is that worship involves much more than just the praise of our lips. It also involves the meditations of our heart and the work that we do. Our worship consists not only of acknowledging God's nature, attributes, and character with our praise and thanksgiving, but also in our work, our good deeds, our service, and our lifestyle. When we live and walk in "Eden," *everything* we say, think, and do becomes an act of worship.

> **W**ithout praise there is no presence, and without presence there is no worship.

❖ PRINCIPLES ❖

1. If we desire to live a *kabod* lifestyle, we must learn to cultivate a continual environment of praise.

2. As we learn to exercise our personal praise ministry, we can create "islands of Eden" around us wherever we go.

3. Praise establishes an environment in which God is pleased to dwell.

4. Praise is agreeing with God concerning Himself.

5. True praise comes only from a humble heart that is focused on God.

6. Wholehearted praise maintains God's presence.

7. We do not invite God's presence in, or even pray His presence in, as much as we *praise* His presence into a place.

8. Worship results when God accepts our praise and manifests His presence.

9. If it is true that we seek God's presence, it is equally true that He seeks worshipers.

10. Worship takes place when God dwells in our praise and begins to mingle with us.

11. Without praise there is no presence, and without presence there is no worship.

12. When we live and walk in "Eden," *everything* we say, think, and do becomes an act of worship.

Chapter Seven

Squeezing the Glory Out

Mine be the travail, and Thine be the glory![1]

Embracing the Pleasure of Pressure

More often than not, the full glory of a thing is not readily apparent at first glance. It is hidden beneath the surface. Glory comes out through a process that inevitably and permanently alters its container. Consider an orange, for example. What is the true glory of an orange? Its bright orange color? Its roundness? The texture of its peel? Although each of these characteristics helps us distinguish an orange from other kinds of fruit, none of them reveals its full essence. The true glory of an orange is its juice.

---

1. Geoffrey Chaucer, "The Knight's Tale," l. 2406, *The Canterbury Tales*, quoted in John Bartlett, *Bartlett's Familiar Quotations*, 16th ed., Justin Kaplan, ed. (New York: Little, Brown and Company, 1992), p. 130:20.

❖ The Glory of Living

How do we get juice from an orange? The only way is to cut open the orange and squeeze the juice out. That process permanently alters the qualities and appearance of the orange. It is impossible to get orange juice without changing the orange. There is no way to bring out the glory of an orange without squeezing it.

In a similar way, God's glory in us is not always readily apparent because it is hidden inside these "jars of clay" that we call our bodies. Bringing out that glory will permanently change the jars containing it.

God's purpose for us is that we become what He created us to be so that His glory hidden in our "jars of clay" can shine forth and bring the light of His true nature to a blind and dark world. In Matthew 5:48 Jesus charged us to "Be perfect, therefore, as your heavenly Father is perfect." You will remember from Chapter Four that the word *perfect* in this verse means "complete" or "mature." We are to be complete and mature just like our heavenly Father: "like Father, like son (or daughter)." The challenge we face is knowing how to become complete. How do we grow to maturity in Christ?

Part of the answer comes in learning simply to trust God to finish what He started. In his letter to the Philippians, Paul encourages us to "[be] confident of this, that He who began a good work in you will carry it on to completion until the day of Christ Jesus" (Phil. 1:6). What God has begun, He will complete. Having called us to salvation in Christ, God will bring us to full maturity in our faith, provided we learn to yield, follow, and obey Him. This is part of what it means to humble ourselves before the Lord. God's part is to bring us to maturity in Christ; that's why He gave us the Holy Spirit. Our part is to listen, trust, and obey. In the rich environment of this relationship, God will bring out His glory that resides within us.

One important principle of maturity that we need to understand is that growth occurs only as we overcome resistance and obstacles. Tests and trials will come—they are an inescapable part of life—and they will make us or break us depending on our attitude toward them. We tend to complain about our trials, but God wants to use them to strengthen us and bring us to maturity. Listen to the wise words of James:

> **Consider it pure joy, my brothers, whenever you face trials of many kinds, because you know that the testing of your faith develops perseverance. Perseverance must finish its work so that you may be mature and complete, not lacking anything....Blessed is the man who perseveres under trial, because when he has stood the test, he will receive the crown of life that God has promised to those who love Him** (James 1:2-4;12).

We can look on our trials with joy when we learn to see beyond the trials themselves to God's purpose to use them to build us up. Tests of our faith develop perseverance, and perseverance leads to maturity and completeness. The climax of this process is when we receive God's promised "crown of life"—the completion of our salvation when we are ushered into God's presence forever.

Regarding this salvation, Peter writes:

> **In this you greatly rejoice, though now for a little while you may have had to suffer grief in all kinds of trials. These have come so that your faith—of greater worth than gold, which perishes even though refined by fire—may be proved genuine and may result in praise, glory and honor when Jesus Christ is revealed. Though you have not seen Him, you love Him; and even though you do not see Him now, you believe in Him and are filled with an inexpressible and glorious joy, for you are receiving the goal of your faith, the salvation of your souls** (1 Peter 1:6-9).

According to Peter, trials refine and purify our faith like fire refines gold. Just as fire burns out the impurities in gold, making it more valuable than before, trials temper and prove the genuineness of our faith. The result of faith tested and proven in this way is "praise, glory, and honor."

Glory Comes Out Under Pressure

It is clear from these Scriptures that trials and testing play a vital role in our spiritual maturity and in preparing us to expose our glory. Have you ever wondered why it seems that every time you solve a problem another is waiting to take its place? It's a matter of glory. Glory comes out under pressure. God uses resistance—problems, trials, tests, obstacles—to "squeeze" His glory out of us. It's when we're under pressure that we reveal what we're really made of.

We rarely grow much during good times. Throughout history, the Church has experienced its greatest periods of growth and effectiveness during hard times, particularly times of persecution. The same is true for each of us as individual believers. We come to know God more during difficult times because it is then that He can most reveal His nature, character, and power. Through hard times God can show us aspects of His nature we would never know otherwise, as well as expose in us glory we never knew was there. In this way God is magnified and glorified before the nations. We show the world how big God is by the trials He brings us through.

In a sense, our life is like a sponge soaked with God's glory that no one can see until we're squeezed to let it out. We're like a tea bag filled with the aromatic leaves of God's life-giving Spirit that cannot come out until we are placed in hot water. We're like a lemon saturated with God's "glory juice" that, once squeezed, can make lemonade to sweeten the world with His presence. No one knows what's inside us until God allows us into situations that put us under pressure. That's when whatever is inside us—our *true* self—comes out.

Pressure is one of the keys to releasing the glory of God in us. If we never faced any challenges we would never grow. If we never had any problems, how would we ever learn that God can solve them? Pressure situations teach us to depend on God because they quickly drive us to the end of our own resources. When we reach the "end of our rope" God is there ready and waiting to deal with the situation and bring out His glory in us. What we see as problems God sees as opportunities to manifest His glory. Our challenge is to learn how to stop looking at our circumstances through our own eyes and start seeing them from God's perspective.

Circumstances are God's gifts to our glory. God brings us into certain circumstances because He wants to show Himself off in our lives. He wants us to expose the glory that is within us, and often uses the situations of life to help us out. Furthermore, as believers we never face anything that hasn't passed through God first. Whatever God allows to come to us is for the purpose of bringing out what's inside. The "problems" we face are in reality opportunities for us to show the world who we really are: children of God and overcomers.

Jesus said, "I have told you these things, so that in Me you may have peace. In this world you will have trouble. But take heart! I have overcome the world" (Jn. 16:33). Through faith in Christ we too will overcome the world. In his first letter the apostle John had a lot to say about overcoming:

> **W**hat we see as problems God sees as opportunities to manifest His glory.

> **I write to you, young men, because you are strong, and the word of God lives in you, and you have overcome the evil one** (1 John 2:14b).

You, dear children, are from God and have overcome them, because the one who is in you is greater than the one who is in the world (1 John 4:4).

For everyone born of God overcomes the world. This is the victory that has overcome the world, even our faith. Who is it that overcomes the world? Only he who believes that Jesus is the Son of God (1 John 5:4-5).

Revelation 12:10-11 speaks of believers overcoming satan, the accuser of the brethren, "by the blood of the Lamb and by the word of their testimony." How often do we give testimonies about our good times? Usually we testify to what God has done for us in difficult times: healing us from illness, giving us victory over the enemy, or bringing us through trials. We never see the glory and power of God more clearly than against the background of trials and obstacles.

From God's perspective there are no problems, only opportunities to reveal His glory. If we are yielded and obedient to Him, the pressure that He allows to come upon us in life will squeeze out the glory that is in us.

Jealous for Glory

One important key to understanding the Bible is to recognize that it is God-centered, not man-centered. Everything in Scripture is presented from the perspective of God's person, purposes, and ways. God is very jealous both for the reputation of His name and for His glory. When He gave the second commandment prohibiting the making of graven images, God said, "I, the Lord your God, am a jealous God" (Ex. 20:5b). Shortly before his death Moses reminded the Israelites, "For the Lord your God is a consuming fire, a jealous God" (Deut. 4:24). God is jealous not in the negative sense of being mistrustful but in the positive sense of being protective and watchful. He is protective of His name and His holiness.

Another way to look at this is to say that God is zealous—ardent—for the integrity of His good name. It is this kind of "jealousy" that Jesus displayed when He overturned the tables of the money changers in the temple and drove them out, saying, "Is it not written: 'My house will be called a house of prayer for all nations'? But you have made it 'a den of robbers'" (Mk. 11:17). Commenting on this event years later, John wrote, "His disciples remembered that it is written: 'Zeal for Your house will consume me'" (Jn. 2:17). This is a quote from Psalm 69:9.

God is very jealous for His name. He wants His glory to fill the whole earth so that all people everywhere will know that He is God. Everything that God does toward man is redemptive in nature. Even His judgment has a redemptive purpose behind it. God is omnipotent, and nothing can prevent Him from accomplishing His purposes. If this is true, then why does God so often allow trials, hardships, and obstacles to come in the way of His people? Why doesn't He just sweep them away and accomplish His will quickly and directly? The answer has to do with His glory. God's power, nature, character, and glory can be seen by the most people as He works through those difficulties. When people see God working *through* and overcoming obstacles, they will know He is God and will give Him glory.

"I Am the Lord"

One of the best biblical examples of God working this way is the account in Exodus of His deliverance of the Israelites from slavery in Egypt. God could simply have brought them out immediately and directly, but that way neither the Israelites nor the Egyptians would have come to know Him in His glory. For that reason, God chose to work *through* the resistance of Pharaoh and his advisors. By the time it was all over, both Israel and Egypt knew that God was the Lord.

Throughout the exodus story God reveals this as His purpose.

I will take you as My own people, and I will be your God. Then you will know that I am the Lord your God, who brought you out from under the yoke of the Egyptians (Exodus 6:7).

And the Egyptians will know that I am the Lord when I stretch out My hand against Egypt and bring the Israelites out of it (Exodus 7:5).

And I will harden Pharaoh's heart, and he will pursue them. But I will gain glory for Myself through Pharaoh

> **and all his army, and the Egyptians will know that I am the Lord...** (Exodus 14:4).

> **The Egyptians will know that I am the Lord when I gain glory through Pharaoh, his chariots and his horsemen** (Exodus 14:18).

> **They will know that I am the Lord their God, who brought them out of Egypt so that I might dwell among them. I am the Lord their God** (Exodus 29:46).

This self-revelation of God is evident even when He calls to Moses from the midst of the burning bush.

> **I am the God of your father, the God of Abraham, the God of Isaac and the God of Jacob...I have indeed seen the misery of My people in Egypt. I have heard them crying out because of their slave drivers, and I am concerned about their suffering. So I have come down to rescue them from the hand of the Egyptians and to bring them up out of that land into a good and spacious land, a land flowing with milk and honey...And now the cry of the Israelites has reached Me, and I have seen the way the Egyptians are oppressing them. So now, go. I am sending you to Pharaoh to bring My people the Israelites out of Egypt** (Exodus 3:6a;7-8a;9-10).

When Moses asks how he should answer the Israelites when they ask him who sent him, God replies:

> **I Am Who I Am. This is what you are to say to the Israelites: "I Am has sent me to you."...Say to the Israelites, "The Lord, the God of your fathers—the God of Abraham, the God of Isaac and the God of Jacob—has sent me to you." This is My name forever, the name by which I am to be remembered from generation to generation** (Exodus 3:14-15).

Then God gives Moses a hint of what to expect when he returns to Egypt:

> **But I know that the king of Egypt will not let you go unless a mighty hand compels him. So I will stretch out My hand and strike the Egyptians with all the wonders that I will perform among them. After that, he will let you go** (Exodus 3:19-20).

Moses, however, was afraid to manifest his glory. He thought the job was too big, the assignment too great. He even tried to talk God into sending someone else. Like Moses, 99 percent of all the people on earth are afraid to manifest their glory. Just as Moses made excuses to God as to why he could not do what God asked, so do 99 percent of the people on earth. God responded by providing Moses with the secret for exposing his glory: "I will be with you" (Ex. 3:12a). The very thing that Cain lost, Moses found: the presence of God. **The secret to manifesting glory is the presence of God.**

"Squeeze Play"

When Moses arrived in Egypt he went to Pharaoh and put the squeeze on the king: "This is what the Lord, the God of Israel, says: 'Let My people go, so that they may hold a festival to Me in the desert' " (Ex. 5:1b). Pharaoh, however, squeezed right back: "Who is the Lord, that I should obey Him and let Israel go? I do not know the Lord and I will not let Israel go" (Ex. 5:2). Then, instead of lightening the burden of the Israelites, he increased it by refusing to supply them with straw for the bricks they made, as he had done previously. Now the Israelites had to find their own straw, yet continue to make the same quota of bricks.

This development caused the Israelite foremen to rail angrily at Moses and Aaron: "May the Lord look upon you and judge you! You have made us a stench to Pharaoh and his officials and have put a sword in their hand to kill us" (Ex. 5:21). Moses, in turn, complained to God: "O Lord, why have You brought trouble upon this people? Is this why You sent me? Ever since I went to Pharaoh to speak in Your name, he has brought trouble upon this people, and You have not rescued Your people at all" (Ex. 5:22b-23). By all appearances, round one of this "squeeze play" had gone to Pharaoh.

In truth, however, God was just getting started. "Then the Lord said to Moses, 'Now you will see what I will do to Pharaoh: Because of My mighty hand he will let them go; because of My mighty hand he will drive them out of his country'" (Ex. 6:1). Now the great contest began in earnest as God Himself put the squeeze on Pharaoh.

Pharaoh's initial response is not surprising. After all, he did not yet know the God of Israel and had no reason to fear Him or obey His command to let the Israelites go. The word *pharaoh* literally means "great house," and originally referred to the king's palace, only later becoming a title for the king himself. In a country where the people had a god for just about everything, it was only natural that over the generations rulers with such absolute power as the pharaohs enjoyed would themselves be regarded as gods. The Egyptian people believed that the pharaohs were actually descended from the gods, so by the time of the exodus they not only followed and obeyed Pharaoh but worshiped him as well.

God always wants to expose His glory so that people can see and know Him. Pharaoh's stubbornness and resistance gave God the perfect opportunity. The contest that followed was a matchup between the false "gods" of Egypt and the God of Israel, the one true God. Since Pharaoh did not know the Lord, God said, "Here's a great opportunity for this 'little fellow' to meet Me, so I'm going to squeeze him and let him bring My glory out." God then sent a series of ten plagues on Egypt, each

> **God always wants to expose His glory so that people can see and know Him.**

one more severe than the preceding one, and each one a direct attack on one of the so-called "gods" of Egypt, including Pharaoh himself.

Tightening His Grip

Through Moses, God turned the waters of the Nile River to blood, killing all life in it. (The Egyptians worshiped the Nile as a god.) Pharaoh hardened his heart and would not let the Israelites go. God squeezed a little harder, inundating Egypt with frogs. At first, Pharaoh seemed to give in, then changed his mind and hardened his heart once again. Then God sent a plague of gnats, followed by a plague of flies. Flies were everywhere: in eyes, ears, and mouths, in wash basins, in cooking pots. After the flies, Pharaoh caught Moses and said, "Okay, okay, your God wins the 'fly war,' now pray for Him to take them away." God's squeeze play was beginning to hurt. Moses prayed and God took away the flies, but Pharaoh again hardened his heart and refused to release the Israelites.

The next plague killed all the livestock of the Egyptians—but did not touch those of the Israelites. God followed that with an epidemic of painful boils that attacked both people and animals. Once again, Pharaoh would not budge. This time, however, the Scripture says, "But the Lord hardened Pharaoh's heart and he would not listen to Moses and Aaron, just as the Lord had said to Moses" (Ex. 9:12). This does not mean that God took over Pharaoh's mind so that he could not change, but that God allowed him to continue to have a stubborn heart.

At this point, God appealed to Pharaoh's common sense.

Then the Lord said to Moses, "Get up early in the morning, confront Pharaoh and say to him, 'This is what the Lord, the God of the Hebrews, says: Let My people go, so that they may worship Me, or this time I will send the full force of My plagues against you and against your officials

and your people, so you may know that there is no one like Me in all the earth. For by now I could have stretched out My hand and struck you and your people with a plague that would have wiped you off the earth. But I have raised you up for this very purpose, that I might show you My power and that My name might be proclaimed in all the earth (Exodus 9:13-16).

Pharaoh refused to listen, however, so the Lord sent a great hailstorm that destroyed crops and killed any animals left in the fields. Following the hail was a plague of locusts that devoured the fruit on the trees and whatever crops were left in the fields. Three days of darkness throughout Egypt (except in Goshen, where the Israelites lived) came on the heels of the locusts.

By this time Pharaoh was beginning to weaken. After each plague he got closer and closer to actually letting the Israelites go, but always at the last minute steeled his resolve and hardened his heart again. In fact, after the plague of darkness, the Scripture says once again that God hardened Pharaoh's heart. This time, Pharaoh was so obstinate that he threatened to kill Moses if Moses came to him again.

It is ironic that even as Pharaoh threatened Moses with death, God was preparing to send the tenth and final plague: the death of all the firstborn in Egypt. The Israelites were spared this plague by spreading lamb's blood on the doorposts of their houses, remaining indoors, and eating a meal of lamb, bitter herbs, and unleavened bread, even while dressed for travel at a moment's notice. This was the institution of the Passover, which would forever commemorate God's deliverance of Israel from Egyptian slavery.

God poured on the pressure—the final squeeze. That night someone died in every Egyptian household, including Pharaoh's. The king had finally had enough.

During the night Pharaoh summoned Moses and Aaron and said, "Up! Leave my people, you and the Israelites! Go, worship the Lord as you have requested. Take your flocks and herds, as you have said, and go. And also bless me." The Egyptians urged the people to hurry and leave the country. "For otherwise," they said, "we will all die!" (Exodus 12:31-33).

When the time came, the Israelites were not simply set free; they were practically driven out of Egypt! Pharaoh and the Egyptian people could no longer deny the power and glory of God. Whether they liked it or not, they now knew who He was. As for the Israelites, they now knew who God was, too. He was *their* God, their Savior and deliverer. They knew His power and had seen His glory. God "squeezed" Egypt and His glory came out.

The Last Straw

Some people just don't know when to quit. That was Pharaoh's problem. There comes a time to stop resisting God, but Pharaoh missed it. He could have lived happily ever after without his Hebrew slaves. Instead of leaving well enough alone he pressed the issue to the point of disaster. The dust hadn't even settled from the Israelites' departure when the Egyptian king changed his mind again. Once more Pharaoh set himself in opposition to God's will for the Israelites. In doing so he played right into God's hands.

Then the Lord said to Moses, "Tell the Israelites to turn back and encamp near Pi Hahiroth, between Migdol and the sea. They are to encamp by the sea, directly opposite Baal Zephon. Pharaoh will think, 'The Israelites are wandering around the land in confusion, hemmed in by the desert.' And I will harden Pharaoh's heart, and he will pursue them. But I will gain glory for Myself through Pharaoh and all his army, and the Egyptians will know that I am the Lord." So the Israelites did this (Exodus 14:1-4).

Notice the connection here. First, God said, "I will harden Pharaoh's heart," and then, "I will gain glory for Myself through Pharaoh." Why? So that "the Egyptians will know that I am the Lord." God was going to use Pharaoh's stubbornness to expose His glory so that Pharaoh and the rest of the Egyptians would know that He was God.

Although Pharaoh had seen abundant evidence of the power and glory of God, apparently he hadn't learned much. The stage was being set for the last straw, the final stroke.

> **When the king of Egypt was told that the people had fled, Pharaoh and his officials changed their minds about them and said, "What have we done? We have let the Israelites go and have lost their services!" So he had his chariot made ready and took his army with him. He took six hundred of the best chariots, along with all the other chariots of Egypt, with officers over all of them. The Lord hardened the heart of Pharaoh king of Egypt, so that he pursued the Israelites, who were marching out boldly. The Egyptians—all Pharaoh's horses and chariots, horsemen and troops—pursued the Israelites and overtook them as they camped by the sea near Pi Hahiroth, opposite Baal Zephon** (Exodus 14:5-9).

When the Israelites spotted the Egyptian army pursuing them, they were terrified and complained to Moses, blaming him for bringing them out into the desert only to face death. Moses' response revealed his complete and utter trust in the Lord.

> **Moses answered the people, "Do not be afraid. Stand firm and you will see the deliverance the Lord will bring you today. The Egyptians you see today you will never see again. The Lord will fight for you; you need only to be still"** (Exodus 14:13-14).

Then, at God's command, Moses held his staff out over the sea. God parted the waters and the Israelites crossed over on dry land.

When the Egyptians attempted to follow, God brought the waters together again, drowning them in the midst. Not one escaped.

God exposed His glory and, as a result, the Egyptians and especially the Israelites came to know Him.

And when the Israelites saw the great power the Lord displayed against the Egyptians, the people feared the Lord and put their trust in Him and in Moses His servant (Exodus 14:31).

A God-Centered Perspective

"Stand firm and...see the [Lord's] deliverance" is good counsel for all of us. Sometimes the best way to bring out the glory of God in us is for someone to stand in our way. Pharaoh stood in the way of the Israelites, and Moses told them to "stand firm and you will see the deliverance the Lord will bring to you today." Whenever we face trials or obstacles that hold us back from becoming what we were born to be, it may be time for us to "stand firm and see" as God blows holes in the walls that block our way.

Sometimes God will "squeeze" us by allowing trials, hardships, and obstacles to pressure us, not only to test, temper, purify, and strengthen our faith, but also to bring out His glory in us so that others can see Him. We need to learn to look at problems the way God does—as opportunities for the glory to come out. As believers we are "jars of clay" that contain God's glory, and squeezing us will bring it out. If life has you "in a squeeze," don't despair; that's a good place to be. Trust that God wants to manifest His glory in and through you. Let life's pressures squeeze the glory out of you so it permeates the environment around you with the sweet fragrance of God's presence.

This will call for a complete change of viewpoint for many of us. So often we look at our Christian lives from a self-centered perspective, always seeking ways to be blessed or healed or comforted, or thinking in terms of what God can do for us. If we want to become all we were born to be and see God's glory manifested in and through us, we must adjust to a God-centered perspective on life. As believers and disciples, our lives are not our own. We belong to God and He has the absolute right to use us according to His will and purpose in order to reveal Himself and make Himself known to people who need to know Him.

We need to be ready and willing to be "squeezed" for God's glory. Sometimes squeezing hurts, but the results and the rewards are well worth the pain. God will show up and people will see and know who He is. If we need encouragement and an example of a life lived from a God-centered perspective, we need look no farther than the life of Jesus.

> **Let life's pressures squeeze the glory out of you so it permeates the environment around you with the sweet fragrance of God's presence.**

❖ PRINCIPLES ❖

1. Glory comes out under pressure.

2. We show the world how big God is by the trials He brings us through.

3. What we see as problems God sees as opportunities to manifest His glory.

4. God is very jealous both for the reputation of His name and for His glory.

5. When people see God working through and overcoming obstacles, they will know He is God and will give Him glory.

6. God always wants to expose His glory so that people can see and know Him.

7. Sometimes God will "squeeze" us by allowing trials, hardships, and obstacles to pressure us, not only to test, temper, purify, and strengthen our faith, but also to bring out His glory in us so that others can see Him.

8. Let life's pressures squeeze the glory out of you so it permeates the environment around you with the sweet fragrance of God's presence.

9. If we want to become all we were born to be and see God's glory manifested in and through us, we must adjust to a God-centered perspective on life.

10. We need to be ready and willing to be "squeezed" for God's glory.

Chapter Eight

Jesus—Revealing God's Glory

The purpose of life is to reveal our glory.

The world defines success in many ways: wealth, fame, power, influence. For some, success means having a better job, a higher salary, a bigger house, or a nicer car than the neighbors do. Others consider themselves successful when they have reached the top of the social ladder and are attending all the "right" parties and hobnobbing with all the "right" people.

While there is nothing inherently wrong with material prosperity or social advancement, we must be careful not to let the desire for them consume us. Many people pursue these things as the end goal of life, only to find them empty. Contrary to what the world tells us, there is more to life than possessions and social status. According to the four Gospels, Jesus had more to say about money, possessions, and our attitude toward them than about any other subject. One day He warned His listeners, "Watch out! Be on your guard against all kinds of greed; a man's life does not consist in the abundance of his possessions" (Lk. 12:15). Yet, many believers pursue these things with the same intensity and drive as non-believers, as if there was no other purpose in life.

Jesus gives us the perfect model of a truly successful life. If we were trying to summarize in one sentence the life of our Lord, we could do no better than what He Himself said in a prayer to His Father:

I have brought You glory on earth by completing the work You gave Me to do (John 17:4).

Notice that Jesus exposed God's glory not through praise and worship, but through His *work*. For Jesus, glorifying God meant being obedient and faithful to finish the mission He had received from His Father. Everything Jesus did on earth—His preaching and teaching, His healing and other miracles—pointed toward the one defining event in His life: the cross. Jesus' prayer in the 17th chapter of John came on the night before He died; He was arrested shortly afterward. His next stop was Calvary.

Jesus was born for the cross. That was where the fullness of His glory was revealed. Jesus was "the Lamb of God, who takes away the sin of the world" (Jn. 1:29b), but He would not be fully revealed as that Lamb until He hung on the cross. Jesus began His prayer with the words, "Father, the time has come. Glorify Your Son, that Your Son may glorify You" (Jn. 17:1). Jesus had finished His work and the time had come for His full glory to be revealed. It was as if Jesus was saying, "Everything up to now has been merely a prelude. Walking on water, multiplying fish and bread, healing the sick, raising the dead—none of that has revealed My *full* weight. My *true* glory is still hidden. I have waited My whole life for *this* hour, because now the people are going to see who I *really* am! And when they see who *I* really am, they will know who *You* really are also!"

Calvary was Jesus' finest hour. From the cross He gave testimony to His completed work when He cried out, "It is finished" (Jn. 19:30b).

Through His obedience Jesus glorified both Himself and His Father. Hebrews 5:8 says, "Although He was a son, He learned obedience from what He suffered." Quoting from what may be one of the earliest Christian hymns in existence, Paul wrote to the Philippians concerning Jesus:

> **And being found in appearance as a man, He humbled Himself and became obedient to death—even death on a cross! Therefore God exalted Him to the highest place and gave Him the name that is above every name, that at the name of Jesus every knee should bow, in heaven and on earth and under the earth, and every tongue confess that Jesus Christ is Lord, to the glory of God the Father** (Philippians 2:8-11).

The cross made possible the empty tomb. Jesus had to die in order to rise again. Calvary revealed Jesus as the Lamb of God who took away the sin of the world, while the Resurrection revealed Him as Christ the Lord, whose name is above every other name. God the Father exalted and glorified His Son because Jesus glorified His Father by completing the work He was sent to do. This was the pattern of Jesus' life. The Gospel of John shows clearly how Jesus revealed God's glory in everything He did and said.

"We Have Seen His Glory"

From the very beginning of his Gospel, John wastes no time declaring who Jesus is:

> **In the beginning was the Word, and the Word was with God, and the Word was God. He was with God in the beginning. Through Him all things were made; without Him nothing was made that has been made. In Him was life, and that life was the light of men. The light shines in the darkness, but the darkness has not understood it** (John 1:1-5).

❖ The Glory of Living

Jesus Christ was the full image and expression of God in human, bodily form. From this brief passage alone we learn that Jesus *was* God and was *with* God from the beginning, that He was the agent through whom all things were created, and that He is the source of life, not just physical life, but also spiritual life.

Jesus came in the flesh to show us what God is like. For example, God is the Life-Giver. So is Jesus.

For just as the Father raises the dead and gives them life, even so the Son gives life to whom He is pleased to give it (John 5:21).

I [Jesus] give them eternal life, and they shall never perish; no one can snatch them out of My hand (John 10:28).

For You granted Him [Jesus] authority over all people that He might give eternal life to all those You have given Him (John 17:2).

Sin brings death. Jesus is the Savior who came to bring us life. In giving us life, Jesus reveals the Father so we can know what He is like. He makes it possible for us to become children of God.

Yet to all who received Him, to those who believed in His name, He gave the right to become children of God— children born not of natural descent, nor of human decision or a husband's will, but born of God (John 1:12-13).

God took on human form so we could see for ourselves the full expression of His nature and character. He became like us so that we could once again become like Him. Jesus was the full manifestation of God's glory in the flesh. His life is an example of what we should be in our "jars of clay."

The Word became flesh and made His dwelling among us. We have seen His glory, the glory of the One and Only, who came from the Father, full of grace and truth....No

one has ever seen God, but God the One and Only, who is at the Father's side, has made Him known (John 1:14,18).

The phrase "made His dwelling" translates the Greek word *skenoo*, which literally means to "tabernacle" or "spread one's tent." When Jesus came in the flesh He "tabernacled," or "pitched His tent" in our midst so that we could see Him and know Him. As the "One and Only" Son of the Father, Jesus exposed God's glory. John is saying that Jesus showed us what the Source is like. By uncovering the "full weight" of the Father, He revealed to us the character of God.

What is the character of God? He is "full of grace and truth." The Greek word for grace is *charis*, which also means "blessing," "favor," and "gift." It is where we get the word *charisma*. One of the characteristics of God is that He bestows blessings, extends favor, and gives gifts to His people. Christ is the mediator through whom they come. Paul wrote to the Ephesians, "But to each one of us grace has been given as Christ apportioned it. This is why it says: 'When He ascended on high, He led captives in his train and gave gifts to men'" (Eph. 4:7-8).

God is also full of truth. Not only is He the *source* of truth; He *is* Truth. Objectively, this means that God is the core reality that underlies everything that exists, both physical and spiritual, visible and invisible. Subjectively, it means that God is free of any and all pretence, falsehood, and deceit. God's truth is sincerity and integrity of character. He never lies and always keeps His promises. God is utterly trustworthy and absolutely holy. In fact, holiness is another way to define truth.

James described the God of grace and truth this way: "Every good and perfect gift is from above, coming down from the Father of the heavenly lights, who does not change like shifting shadows" (Jas. 1:17). God is grace, the giver of "every good and perfect gift," and He is truth, unchanging and without a hint or shadow of falseness. These same characteristics describe Jesus. As Jesus Himself told Philip, "Anyone who has seen Me has seen the Father" (Jn. 14:9b). When we look at Jesus, we see God.

Water, Wine, and Glory

One of the ways Jesus revealed the Father and Himself was through the miracles He performed. I think it is particularly significant that the setting for His first miracle was not a public street or an open hillside where it was witnessed by hundreds of people, but a private home in the midst of the joyous festivities of a family wedding celebration. The scenario is intimate and very ordinary: Jesus is attending a wedding in the town of Cana in Galilee, along with His disciples and His mother, Mary. Cana was located about eight miles north of Nazareth, where Jesus grew up. The wine has run out and the hosts are facing a deeply embarrassing social crisis. Mary appeals to her Son for help (see Jn. 2:1-3).

In those days and in that culture wedding celebrations commonly lasted several days, even as long as a week. The hosts were responsible for making sure that enough food and wine were available at all times for all their guests. A failure in hospitality was a serious shortcoming in that culture and could cause damage to a family's reputation that would endure for years.

Why was Mary so concerned that she sought Jesus' help? Many Bible scholars believe that the hosts of the wedding celebration were blood relatives of Mary and Jesus. This was "family," and they were in need. At first, however, Jesus appears reluctant to intervene. Nevertheless, His mother instructs the servants to do whatever Jesus says. What happens next is very low-key and takes place with no drama, fanfare, or publicity.

Nearby stood six stone water jars, the kind used by the Jews for ceremonial washing, each holding from twenty to thirty gallons. Jesus said to the servants, "Fill the jars with water"; so they filled them to the brim. Then He told them, "Now draw some out and take it to the master of the

banquet." They did so, and the master of the banquet tasted the water that had been turned into wine. He did not realize where it had come from, though the servants who had drawn the water knew. Then he called the bridegroom aside and said, "Everyone brings out the choice wine first and then the cheaper wine after the guests have had too much to drink; but you have saved the best till now." This, the first of His miraculous signs, Jesus performed in Cana of Galilee. He thus revealed His glory, and His disciples put their faith in Him (John 2:6-11).

Just like that, Jesus averted a social embarrassment and preserved a family's reputation in the community. By doing so, He demonstrated the deeply personal interest that God takes in even the most ordinary affairs of our lives. In the Bible, wine is often used as a symbol for the Spirit of God. The new wine from Jesus was superior to the wine that had run out. In the same way, the life in the Spirit which we receive from Christ is far superior to the old life of sin, or even "religion" that has proved inadequate. Verse 11 explains Jesus' primary motivation for turning the water into wine: to reveal His glory so that His disciples would believe in Him.

There are at least three truths or principles we can draw from this story.

1. *Sometimes God allows things to "run out" in order to reveal His glory.* Because the wine ran out, Jesus had an opportunity to reveal Himself and build the faith of His disciples. If you start to run out of stuff—the water runs out, or the money runs out, or a friendship runs out—don't panic. Just say, "God, there must be something about Yourself that You want to show me; that's why things have run out. Reveal Your glory."

2. *When life throws you a curve, remember that it's a glory curve.* If we are followers of Christ, life can never really

catch us on our blind side because God knows everything. So, if you see a curve ahead, don't panic; God is waiting just around the bend. The glory is about to come up.

3. *Glory always reveals that which is better than what we had before.* The earlier wine at the Cana wedding may have been good, but Jesus' wine was better. Isn't God beautiful? Jesus didn't simply turn water into wine; He saved an entire family's reputation. The point I'm

> **Glory always reveals that which is better than what we had before.**

making is, if you think that where you are and what you have are good, "you ain't seen nothing yet!" The best is yet to come. Glory comes out under pressure, and glory brings out the very best there is.

Like Father, Like Son

One of the reasons Jesus came into conflict so often with the Pharisees and other religious leaders was their resentment and bitter disagreement with His bold claim to be the Son of God. Because they were spiritually blind and did not believe Him, they considered His claim to be blasphemy. They particularly resented the closeness and oneness Jesus claimed to have with His Father.

The eighth chapter of John contains an extended debate between Jesus and the Pharisees in which Jesus makes several statements that reveal much about His relationship to His Father. When His opponents challenged the validity of His testimony, Jesus said,

Even if I testify on My own behalf, My testimony is valid, for I know where I came from and where I am going. But you have no idea where I come from or where I am going.

You judge by human standards; I pass judgment on no one. But if I do judge, My decisions are right, because I am not alone. I stand with the Father, who sent Me. In your own Law it is written that the testimony of two men is valid. I am one who testifies for Myself; My other witness is the Father, who sent Me...You do not know Me or My Father...If you knew Me, you would know My Father also (John 8:14-18;19b).

Twice, Jesus says, "the Father...sent Me." He also says that the Father is a witness to what Jesus says about Himself. Jesus considers that He and His Father are one: "If you knew Me, you would know My Father also." Like Father, like Son.

A little later Jesus said,

When you have lifted up the Son of Man, then you will know that I am the one I claim to be and that I do nothing on My own but speak just what the Father has taught Me. The one who sent Me is with Me; He has not left Me alone, for I always do what pleases Him (John 8:28-29).

Jesus was so close to His Father that He did nothing on His own, but only what His Father taught Him and told Him to do. The Father and the Son enjoyed inseparable fellowship with each other.

When the Pharisees claimed God as their Father, Jesus replied,

If God were your Father, you would love Me, for I came from God and now am here. I have not come on My own; but He sent Me (John 8:42).

Jesus came from God to the earth, not on His own initiative, but at the bidding of His Father.

Summing it all up, Jesus made the boldest statements of all:

I am not seeking glory for Myself; but there is one who seeks it, and He is the judge....If I glorify Myself, My glory

means nothing. My Father, whom you claim as your God, is the one who glorifies Me….I tell you the truth…before Abraham was born, I am! (John 8:50,54,58)

Jesus understood that apart from the Father His glory was nothing. He was saying, "If I were to boast about Myself, that would only bring forth the flesh nature, which is not the glory that God desires. However, the Father is My Source, and He glorifies Me; He reveals the full expression of My life. I am here not to expose Myself, but My Father." When we look at Jesus, we see God.

It's Not About Lazarus, but About God

One day when Jesus received word that His dear friend Lazarus of Bethany was very sick He said, "This sickness will not end in death. No, it is for God's glory so that God's Son may be glorified through it" (Jn. 11:4). Yet, even though it was Lazarus' sisters, Mary and Martha, who had sent word to Jesus and were hoping and expecting Him to come, Jesus delayed His departure for two days. By the time He and His disciples arrived in Bethany, Lazarus was already dead.

When Martha heard that Jesus had come, she confronted Him.

"Lord…if You had been here, my brother would not have died. But I know that even now God will give You whatever you ask." Jesus said to her, "Your brother will rise again." Martha answered, "I know he will rise again in the resurrection at the last day." Jesus said to her, "I am the resurrection and the life. He who believes in Me will live, even though he dies; and whoever lives and believes in Me will never die. Do you believe this?" "Yes, Lord," she told Him, "I believe that You are the Christ, the Son of God, who was to come into the world" (John 11:21-27).

When Jesus said, "I am the resurrection and the life," He was revealing both His own nature and that of His Father. God alone has the power to give life, and He alone has the ability to raise the dead.

A short time later, everyone gathered at Lazarus' tomb, and Jesus ordered the stone taken away from its entrance. When Martha objected because of the odor the body would have after being dead four days, Jesus answered, "Did I not tell you that if you believed, you would see the glory of God?" (Jn. 11:40) Then He called to Lazarus to come out. The dead man came out and everyone was astonished. As a result of this miracle, "many of the Jews who had come to visit Mary, and had seen what Jesus did, put their faith in Him" (Jn. 11:45). Jesus revealed the Father, and God was glorified.

So often as believers we serve God because of the good things He does for us and forget that life is not about blessing, but about glory. God's glory shines the brightest in the midst of dark times and when it comes out under pressure. God wants to expose Himself through us, and He doesn't get much exposure during good times. This may be a difficult truth to accept, but it is a much-needed balance to the "bless me" club. God's glory is of supreme importance, and sometimes He is glorified most in and through our hard times. Jesus could have gone to Lazarus earlier and healed him before he died, but God's glory was put on greater display by raising Lazarus from the dead. By His actions Jesus was saying, "This isn't about Lazarus, but about God." In raising Lazarus, Jesus glorified the Father and was Himself glorified. When we look at Jesus, we see God.

God's Purpose for Mankind Is Glory

God has a reason for everything He does and a purpose for everything He created. He wants every creature to manifest its glory—to expose its true nature. The glory of a bird is to fly, and a fish, to swim. The glory of man is to bring forth fruit that exposes God's glory.

Jesus said,

> **I am the true vine and My Father is the gardener. He cuts off every branch in Me that bears no fruit, while every branch that does bear fruit He prunes so that it will be even more fruitful....Remain in Me, and I will remain in you. No branch can bear fruit by itself; it must remain in the vine. Neither can you bear fruit unless you remain in Me. I am the vine; you are the branches. If a man remains in Me and I in him, he will bear much fruit; apart from Me you can do nothing....This is to My Father's glory, that you bear much fruit, showing yourselves to be My disciples** (John 15:1-2;4-5;8).

Jesus is the "true vine." The glory of a vine is to support and give life to the branches through the sap that flows. We are the branches. The glory of a branch is to bear fruit. It is to the Father's glory not that we sing or worship or have prayer meetings, but that we bring forth fruit. Another word for fruit is productivity. We bring glory to God when we make something productive and worthwhile of our lives. This means finding what we were born to do and doing it.

If fruit means productivity, then productivity means *work*. Remember Jesus' words to His Father: "I have brought You glory on earth by completing the work You gave Me to do" (Jn. 17:4). There is nothing in that verse about praise, prayer, singing, or any other "religious" activity. God's glory came out in the work that Jesus did. Just like Jesus, we glorify God in and through *our* work; that's how He designed us. Man's original role in the Garden of Eden was as a *worker*, overseeing and caring for the garden and all of the lower created order. When we bear fruit (our work), we expose God's glory and prove that we belong to Him.

We don't bring out glory on Sunday, or Saturday, or whatever other day we may worship; we bring out glory in our job or profession on the rest of the days of the week. Glory comes out in our *work*, not in our worship. Our glory is doing the work we were born to do because that reveals who we really are. Revealing who we really are also exposes God's glory within us and makes it possible for others to look at our lives and see who He really is.

> **T**he glory of man is to bring forth fruit that exposes God's glory.

The Glory of Oneness

Jesus' greatest desire for His followers was that they would come to know and experience the same oneness that He and His Father enjoyed. This oneness was the dominating theme of the last recorded prayer of Jesus prior to His crucifixion.

> **And now, Father, glorify Me in Your presence with the glory I had with You before the world began....All I have is Yours, and all You have is Mine. And glory has come to Me through them....My prayer is not for them alone. I pray also for those who will believe in Me through their message, that all of them may be one, Father, just as You are in Me and I am in You. May they also be in Us so that the world may believe that You have sent Me. I have given them the glory that You gave Me, that they may be one as We are one: I in them and You in Me. May they be brought to complete unity to let the world know that You sent Me and have loved them even as You have loved Me. Father, I want those You have given Me to be with Me where I am, and to see My glory, the glory You have given Me because You loved Me before the creation of the world** (John 17:5;10;20-24).

The glory of a manufacturer is seen when its product performs as designed and advertised. If the computer on which I write these words executes all of its designs and functions as it is supposed to, it reflects the glory of the computer company whose name it bears. Jesus said that He had received glory through His followers—"glory has come to Me through them"—who *bear His name.* When we successfully carry out the design or purpose of our Manufacturer, we bring glory to His name.

From before the creation of the world, Jesus and His Father were one and Jesus prayed that His followers would share that same oneness. Too often these verses have been used in the wrong way to teach unity. Jesus' primary concern in these verses is not so much *unity* as it is *union.* Just as Jesus and His Father were one in their shared God-nature, so He prayed that His followers "may be one *as We are one.*" Jesus' prayer for us is that we will be brought into "complete unity" with our *own* God-nature. He wants us to know who we *really* are—children made in the "spitting image" of our Father—rather than buying into the lies of who the rest of the world says we are. Jesus said, "I have given them the glory that You gave Me." What is glory? True nature. Jesus gave us the same nature that He and the Father share.

Jesus glorified His Father by completing the work His Father gave Him to do. Everything Jesus did revealed the Father's glory, but nothing more so than His death on the cross and His resurrection. The cross was Jesus' ultimate "work" which fully manifested His glory; it was what He was born to do. In His death and resurrection Jesus fully revealed the Father.

In the same way, *our* work should reveal Jesus in us, who in turn reveals the Father, who is our Source. What we do with our lives should ultimately reveal the full "weight" of God before a watching world. That's what we were born to do. *Glory is manifested through work.*

> **W**hen we successfully carry out the design or purpose of our Manufacturer, we bring glory to His name.

❖   PRINCIPLES   ❖

1. Jesus was the full manifestation of God's glory in the flesh.

2. When we look at Jesus, we see God.

3. Sometimes God allows things to "run out" in order to reveal His glory.

4. When life throws you a curve, remember that it's a glory curve.

5. Glory always reveals that which is better than what we had before.

6. The Christian life is not about blessing, but about glory.

7. God's glory is of supreme importance, and sometimes He is glorified most in and through our hard times.

8. The glory of man is to bring forth fruit that exposes God's glory.

9. Our glory is doing the work we were born to do because that reveals who we really are.

10. When we successfully carry out the design or purpose of our Manufacturer, we bring glory to His name.

11. Glory is manifested through work.

Chapter Nine

Releasing the Glory

What I do is me: for that I came.[1]

In the world of professional basketball there is widespread agreement among coaches, players, and fans alike that Michael Jordan is the best to ever play the game. Season after season he thrilled and awed thousands with his grace, skill, and accuracy. With a basketball in his hands, he was nothing short of a magician. If ever there was anyone who was born for the game, it is he. Nowhere does Michael Jordan's glory shine brighter than on a basketball court.

Although a slight, bespectacled, and unassuming man, Mahatma Gandhi wielded an influence far greater than his physical appearance suggested. Trained as a lawyer, he devoted himself early in his adult life to working for the rights of minorities and the oppressed in his native India. Himself a Hindu, Gandhi nevertheless

---

1. Gerard Manley Hopkins, "As Kingfishers Catch Fire," public domain.

sought ways for people of all religions to live together in peace, and even embraced many of the moral and ethical teachings of Jesus. He was absolutely committed to nonviolence. His example and lifestyle attracted millions of followers and resulted in the independence of India from Great Britain in 1947. Gandhi's glory was to inspire an entire nation of people and bring them into the light of freedom.

Eric Liddell of Scotland won a gold medal in the 400-meter dash at the 1924 Olympic Games in Paris, France. Born in China to missionary parents, he returned to China in 1925 as a missionary himself and served there until he died in a Japanese internment camp in 1945. He used his fame and acclaim as a runner as an opportunity to talk about Christ. At one point, Eric Liddell said, "I believe God made me for a purpose—for China—but He also made me fast, and when I run, I feel His pleasure." Eric Liddell found and exposed his glory, both as an athlete and as a servant of Christ. He knew personally the joy, pleasure, and fulfillment that came from being what he was born to be.

Finding Your Moment of Glory

Your glory is who you really are, the "ultimate you," the true person hidden inside that no one has ever really seen. Your full glory is everything you were born to do that you haven't done yet; everything you've dreamed but haven't accomplished yet. Once recognized and revealed, your full glory will bring to your life a greater sense of purpose, fulfillment, and satisfaction than anything else. As Os Guinness writes in his book, *The Call,* "We human beings are never happier than when we are expressing the deepest gifts that are truly us."[2]

That's what it means to find your glory: to recognize and exercise your gifts, to discover who you are meant to be and what you

---

2.   Os Guinness, *The Call* (Nashville, TN: Word Publishing, a div. of Thomas Nelson, Inc., 1998), p. 45.

are meant to do, and to devote your life and your energy to becoming that person. There must be a moment in life for each of us when we can say, "This is it!"—a moment when we and our glory become "one." It is a time when we get "in sync" with our glory, a time when the printer finally starts talking to the computer. When we reach that place, we will have realized God's purpose for our life. Until then, we have no "right" to die. None of us are supposed to die until we have fully manifested the glory of God trapped inside us.

To glorify someone means to show or manifest everything he expects from you. For example, if my Compaq® laptop computer performs according to the expectations of its manufacturer, it "brings glory" to the Compaq® company. The company is concerned about its reputation because my computer carries the Compaq® name. In the same way, God is concerned about the reputation of His name. As human beings we carry God's name— His image—and He wants us to perform according to His expectations. We do this by fulfilling every design function He built into us and becoming all He planned for us to be.

In the Bible, a person's name was the same as his reputation. Throughout the Scriptures we see examples of God being very jealous for the reputation of His name. Jesus was also jealous for His Father's name:

> **Jesus replied, "The hour has come for the Son of Man to be glorified....Now My heart is troubled, and what shall I say? 'Father, save Me from this hour'? No, it was for this very reason I came to this hour. Father, glorify Your name!" Then a voice came from heaven, "I have glorified it, and will glorify it again"** (John 12:23;27-28).

Jesus knew that His "moment of glory" would be the cross. There He would completely fulfill everything He was born to do. That's why He said, "The hour has come for the Son of Man to be glorified." Until that moment arrived, Jesus had no "right" to die; it was not His time. When Jesus prayed, "Father, glorify Your name," He was saying, "Father, bring out of Me all of Your expectations in order to protect Your reputation." Jesus knew all along that His own death on the cross would be the fulfillment of His prayer. Whenever we pray or sing to God, "Glorify Your name," we are asking for the same thing Jesus did, that God will bring out of us everything He expects of us for the honor of His reputation. We are asking Him to bring us to our "moment of glory."

If we die without finishing what we were born to do, we are messing with God's reputation, because God doesn't fail. He wants us to bring out our full glory; that's part of His purpose for our lives. Understanding this, seeking to follow and obey the Lord, and working to discover and expose our true glory will help keep us alive. God wants us to die empty; He doesn't want us taking any of our glory to the grave. The Gospel writer John mentions several times how Jesus' enemies wanted to seize Him or put Him to death but did not because "His time had not yet come." Jesus' appointed time—His "moment of glory"—came the night He was betrayed, delivered into the hands of His enemies, and crucified. Until then He was safe from their grasp.

I realized years ago that my glory is to help other people discover theirs, and I have not yet completed that assignment. My full glory has not come out thus far, which is why I am confident that it is not time for me to die. I fly over 200,000 miles a year, all over the world, but never fear for my safety because I know my glory. My work is not finished; God is not through with me yet.

> **G**od has
> a "moment
> of glory" for
> each of us.

God has a "moment of glory" for each of us. The substance of our lives is to pursue that moment until He brings us into it. When we have become everything we were born to be; when we have shown the world our full weight, that's when we have glorified God.

Releasing Our Glory Means Showing God to the World

When we release the glory hidden inside us, we put God on display, unveiling His attributes, likeness, character, and attitude before a waiting and watching world. One way we glorify God is by exposing His nature and attributes. This means to pay open tribute to God for all His accomplishments, those He does directly as well as those He performs in and through us. It means giving God credit where credit is due. Any time we receive applause or recognition for an achievement, we should turn right around and return the credit to God. This does not mean denying our gift or ability through which success came, but to simply and honestly acknowledge God as its source and thank Him for His enabling power that made success possible. To do otherwise is to mishandle the glory of God, and that is very dangerous. Remember that God is jealous for the reputation and integrity of His name. He will not tolerate anyone trying to steal His glory.

Another way we glorify God is by displaying His likeness. This means showing the world what God is like. God created us in His own image and likeness. We are the product of His "manufacture." He has stamped us with His name and wants us to function according to His design. His reputation is on the line.

Most of the people in the world cannot see the likeness of God either in themselves or others because sin has blinded their spiritual eyes and marred the image. When we begin to discover and release our glory through the power of God, we will start to reflect the likeness of our Manufacturer. More and more in our daily life and work we will "show off" the traits of our Maker: "love, joy, peace, patience, kindness, goodness, faithfulness, gentleness, and self-control" (Gal. 5:22b-23a). Other people will then be able to look at us and see what God is like.

A third way we glorify God is by displaying His character. When we begin to manifest in our lives the true characteristics of God, other people may begin to confuse us with Him. They may say, "You remind me of God." If they do, don't feel bad; that's a *good* thing for them to say. As long as we keep ourselves humble before God and allow Him to manifest His glory, others will see His character in us: such things as truthfulness, honor, integrity, justice, and holiness. This does not mean we are competing with God. He wants us to expose His character on the earth. God wants other people to be able to see His nature in us so that they will glorify Him.

We also glorify God by showing creation the attitude of God. When the world sees what God is like, they will begin to appreciate the glory of God in the earth. This is the practical side of glory. Many of us are caught up in the idea that to glorify God means coming to church or to synagogue or to the mosque or whatever, and singing songs, praying prayers, and reading from the holy books or scriptures. That is a "religious" concept that misses the point. We do not glorify God by our religious activities, but by displaying His nature, character, and attitude.

This means that we do not glorify God on our worship day, whenever that is, but on our work days. Glory begins on Monday morning when we kick out of that bed even when we don't want to. It starts when we shower, dress, and walk out of the house saying, "I'm going to expose some stuff today. People are going to see the real me." We glorify God by showing His attitude to the world. This means working out our dreams, maximizing our gifts, using our talents, and bringing out all our hidden abilities.

> **W**e do not glorify God by our religious activities, but by displaying His nature, character, and attitude.

Godliness Is a Key to Glory

Finally, we glorify God by revealing the godliness of the Father. This statement really summarizes the others. When we display the attributes, likeness, character, and attitude of God, we are revealing His godliness. If you think about it, "godliness" is a rather frightening word. It literally means "god-likeness." To be godly means to be just like God. Is it possible for human beings to be like God?

Not only is it possible, but the Bible commands it. Godliness is a key to glory, and the key to godliness is a personal love relationship with God by grace through faith in Jesus Christ as Lord. The early church leaders Paul and Peter both emphasized the importance of godliness. For example, Paul wrote to his young protégé Timothy,

> **...that we may live peaceful and quiet lives in all godliness and holiness** (1 Timothy 2:2).

> **Have nothing to do with godless myths and old wives' tales; rather, train yourself to be godly. For physical training is of some value, but godliness has value for all things, holding promise for both the present life and the life to come** (1 Timothy 4:7-8).

> **But you, man of God, flee from all this, and pursue righteousness, godliness, faith, love, endurance and gentleness** (1 Timothy 6:11).

In his second letter, Peter had this to say about godliness:

> **His divine power has given us everything we need for life and godliness through our knowledge of Him who called us by His own glory and goodness. Through these He has given us His very great and precious promises, so that through them you may participate in the divine nature and escape the corruption in the world caused by evil desires. For this very reason, make every effort to add to your faith goodness; and to goodness, knowledge; and to knowledge, self-control; and to self-control, perseverance; and to perseverance, godliness; and to godliness, brotherly kindness; and to brotherly kindness, love** (2 Peter 1:3-7).

Peter says that believers "participate in the divine nature" (that means "glory") and that God "has given us everything we need for life and godliness." That means that if we are believers, God has already given us everything we need to be like Him. He wants us to respond to life not from a human perspective, but from a godly one.

So often we hide behind the statement, "I'm only human." God says, "That's not enough. I want you to be godly like Me." Every day and in every circumstance we should remind people of God: Monday through Friday, on the weekend, on the job, under pressure, when dealing with disappointment, when people mistreat us. The way we respond to the everyday challenges of life should reveal the nature and likeness of God within us. None of us who are believers should ever again use the excuse "I'm only human." We are more than that. We carry God-likeness in our "jars of clay," and we are supposed to let it out.

The Cost of Godliness

Godliness comes at a personal cost, however. We must work hard at it; it won't happen accidentally. Don't forget that the best way to reveal glory is to put it under pressure. Because our glory is hidden, the best way to bring it forth is to make demands on it. An apple seed has to die in order to bring forth the apple tree. The tree is in the seed, but the seed must be crushed to get the tree out of it.

One day Jesus said to His disciples, "The hour has come for the Son of Man to be glorified. I tell you the truth, unless a kernel of wheat falls to the ground and dies, it remains only a single seed. But if it dies, it produces many seeds" (Jn. 12:23-24). That part about dying is the part we don't like to hear. Unless the seed dies, it cannot bring forth the trees trapped inside. Jesus was referring to Himself, saying that He had to die in order to bring forth His glory—the fruit of millions of changed lives. "But I, when I am lifted up from the earth, will draw all men to Myself" (Jn. 12:32). Millions of committed servants of God were in Him, but He had to die to get them out.

Where glory is concerned, don't expect an easy road. Jesus' road to the cross was not easy but it was right; His full glory lay at the end of it. If we want our glory to come out, we've got to get ready for a rough time. Exposing our glory means going public. We have to be willing to step out on a limb, knowing all the time that there will be plenty of people waiting to cut it off behind us. Paul wrote to Timothy, "In fact, everyone who wants to live a godly life in Christ Jesus will be persecuted" (2 Tim. 3:12). It may mean that you will be beaten up on for 20 years, with people attacking you when you're up, kicking you when you're down, and generally messing with your life. If you bear it with dignity and grace, always looking to God for your support, the day will come when all of a sudden people start saying, "I really respect you; you've done well." What they will mean is that they are seeing glory coming out in your life.

In the end, bringing out our full glory will cost us our lives, just as it did Jesus. Our true glory will not come out until it kills us. Glory consumes us; that's why we die when we're finished. We have literally worked ourselves out of life. That's not something for us to fear. After all, the purpose of life is to get rid of our glory. Living is all about glory manifestation.

God created us to expose His purpose in the world. That's what glory does. Paul, the early church leader, wrote to the believers in the city of Ephesus, "His intent was that now, through the church, the manifold wisdom of God should be made known to the rulers and authorities in the heavenly realms, according to His eternal purpose which He accomplished in Christ Jesus our Lord" (Eph. 3:10-11). These verses describe the restoration of God's original purpose for man: that the Church, that body of believers who are the "called out ones," should manifest to the world the wisdom, nature, and glory of God so that men can see and understand His eternal purpose.

There Is No Such Thing as Secret Glory

The glory that God has placed in each of us may be hidden, but it is never invisible. It may not be apparent at first, but when our glory comes out, everyone will see it. There is no such thing as secret glory. Kings and queens do not rule in secret, hidden away somewhere. Their glory is the authority they possess by virtue of their status as members of a royal family, and normally they exercise it in the open. Traditionally, kings and queens have worn a crown made of gold or precious gems that serves as a vivid visual symbol of their authority; the "glory" of their royalty.

God created human beings to be His royal representatives on the earth. "What is man that You take thought of him, and the son of man that You care for him? Yet You have made him a little lower than God, and You crown him with glory and majesty!" (Ps. 8:4-5 NAS) The word *crown* means to "bestow." When God created us, He didn't give us a physical crown to wear but bestowed on us His glory and majesty. This means that God gave us the right and authority to possess His full weight, attributes, and nature. He does not want us to exercise them in secret.

If we could just understand the authority God has given us, what a difference it would make for us tomorrow! No matter where we were—in our car, on the bus, on the job, shopping—we would find ourselves suddenly possessed of a whole new attitude, confidence, joy, and sense of purpose, all because we had finally realized the great treasure from God that fills the "earth suits" we walk around in.

Jesus said:

You are the light of the world. A city set on a hill cannot be hidden; nor does anyone light a lamp and put it under a basket, but on the lampstand, and it gives light to all who are in the house. Let your light shine before men in such a way that they may see your good works,

and glorify your Father who is in heaven (Matthew 5:14-16 NAS).

We are the light of the world, as obvious as a city on top of a hill. God did not put the light in us in order for us to hide it away. Have you ever watched the Olympic torchbearers? A long succession of specially chosen people carries the symbolic flame hundreds of miles before finally lighting the great fire at the Olympic stadium. These flamebearers hold the torch aloft as they run, proudly, openly, and unashamed, so it is clearly seen by everyone watching.

That's the way God wants us to be with our glory. He is saying, "I sent you to earth, and I want the whole world to see what you're carrying." God doesn't want any secret successes; He wants a public display of what He put inside us. He wants the whole world to see what we're really made of. The glory of God cannot be revealed in secret. If we are determined to bring out our glory, we won't be able to hide it.

What Are You Going to Do With Your Glory?

God likes to make a spectacle of obedient people because He knows that they desire His favor above the favor of men. People who obey God will always be criticized by the world because they keep putting themselves on public display, exposing the glory of God. If you don't want to be criticized, then don't try to do anything with your life. The moment you decide to become who you really are, people will begin to talk about you. They will criticize you, slander you, and gossip about you. Why? Because they can see your glory. Most of the world doesn't want to see the glory of God because its brilliance exposes their sinfulness. Sin loves the darkness. You can't criticize what you can't see. If no one is talking about you, maybe it's because you're not doing anything.

Some folks say, "Don't rock the boat." That's why they're not going anywhere. "Nowhere" people don't want you to succeed. They want you to be a failure just like they are. If you want to do something with your life, you've got to break out of the norm, stop listening to pessimists and losers, and rise above the spirit of mediocrity.

Don't sit back and hide your glory. Lay hold of your dreams. Set your goals high. Determine that you are going to move forward into everything God wants you to be. Don't let anyone hold you back. Enroll in that night class. Work hard and study hard to earn that promotion. Open that car repair shop, dress shop, boutique, or hair salon you've always dreamed of. Paint those pictures. Carve those carvings. Write that novel. Compose those songs or poems that are burning inside you. Get them all out until there are none left. Don't let anyone tell you what you cannot do. You are full of potential and possibilities that no one knows about. Don't deprive the world of your glory. The graveyards are already filled with lost dreams, untapped glory, and unrealized potential. Don't add yours to them. Let the glory God has placed in you come out so His glory can fill the earth.

For an artist, a finished painting is glory exposed. When a painter paints the picture he has imagined in his mind, he manifests his glory. Suppose Michelangelo had never painted the Sistine Chapel or sculpted the *Pieta*. What if Leonardo da Vinci had never painted the *Mona Lisa* or the *Last Supper*? What a tragedy for the world! These men left their glory on the earth for the enrichment of future generations.

> **D**on't deprive the world of your glory.

Whenever we attempt to show God's glory, it will frighten us. God's glory will always frighten us; if it doesn't, something is wrong. Bringing out the glory in us is a God-sized assignment. It is much too big for us to do on our own. That's why it frightens us. We may not believe we can possibly do what we were born to do, but that's exactly why we were born to do it. God wants to expose our glory by bringing us into everything He wants us to be and glorify Himself in the process.

Let your light shine so that people will see your works—*your glory*—and glorify the Father. Jesus' light shone most brightly from the cross. Across 2,000 years, millions of people have looked at the glory of Jesus on the cross and have glorified God the Father. During his sermon on the Day of Pentecost, Peter said, "God has made this Jesus, whom you crucified, both Lord and Christ" (Acts 2:36b). Peter was saying to them, "When you killed Him, God exposed Him." Like a rose whose fragrance becomes even stronger when its petals are crushed, Jesus' glory came out when they crushed Him.

What are *you* going to leave behind for the generations to come? Who's going to see *your* glory after you are gone? Will the lingering fragrance of your glory sweeten the earth?

❖ PRINCIPLES ❖

1. Your glory is who you really are, the "ultimate you," the true person hidden inside that no one has ever really seen.

2. We glorify God by exposing His nature and attributes.

3. We glorify God by displaying His likeness.

4. We glorify God by displaying His character.

5. We glorify God by showing creation the attitude of God.

6. We glorify God by revealing the godliness of the Father.

7. Godliness is a key to glory, and the key to godliness is a personal love relationship with God by grace through faith in Jesus Christ as Lord.

8. God created us to expose His purpose in the world.

9. There is no such thing as secret glory.

10. Who's going to see *your* glory after you are gone?

Chapter Ten

The Fragrance of Glory

The good are better made by ill, as odors crushed are sweeter still.[1]

Does a rose smell its own fragrance? Does an orange taste its own juice? Of course not. They are merely exposing their glory. The glory of a rose is its fragrance; that of an orange, its juice. Their glory comes out for someone else's benefit, however. A rose gives off a sweet fragrance not for its own pleasure but for the pleasure of others. An orange produces refreshing juice not for its own enjoyment but for the enjoyment of others.

What the rose and the orange have in common is that to fully expose their glory they must be crushed. A rose smells wonderful on the bush, but crushing the bloom releases the full essence of its

---

1.   Samuel Rogers, "Jacqueline," stanza 3, public domain, quoted in John Bartlett, *Bartlett's Familiar Quotations,* 16th ed., Justin Kaplan, ed. (New York: Little, Brown and Company, 1992), p. 159:10, note 4.

perfume. An orange smells sweet on the tree, but the only way to extract its juice is to crush it. It is only as they are consumed that the rose and the orange fully manifest their glory. The fragrance is not for the rose and the juice is not for the orange. Their glory exists for others.

The same is true with us. Our glory exists not for our own benefit but for others. Just as we would crush a rose to release its fragrance or an orange to extract its juice, God crushes us to squeeze out our glory. We may be uncomfortable with the pressure He applies but God is delighted with the perfume that results. God created us to release His glory in the world and His purpose will not be completed until the whole earth is filled with its fragrance.

Crushing Releases the Glory

Crushing really is the key to releasing the glory of God. If you feel the weight of life crushing you down, don't despair. God will not let it destroy you. Instead, He will cause it to *reveal* you. Pressure brings out what is hidden underneath. Sometimes that means stripping away the old layers of dirt and debris to get down to the original. It's like taking an antique wooden chair that has many coats of paint on it and carefully sanding and stripping those layers away until the glory of the original wood grain is revealed. At first the process looks destructive as you scrape away at the surface. Eventually, however, the old paint yields to the pressure and the chair appears as it did when it was first made. People may then appreciate it in its original glory.

God's purpose is for the world to see us restored to our original glory, the way He created us. To accomplish that He has to squeeze and scrape and press and crush us. There is no other way. In one way or another He has to break our "jars of clay" in order for His fragrant glory to come out. He wants to do with us what the woman in Bethany did when she broke open her alabaster jar of very expensive perfume and poured the ointment on Jesus' head (see Mk. 14:3). The fragrance of the nard permeated the room. While religious-minded people criticized her for her waste, Jesus commended her for her love. God wants to break open our "jar" so the sweet aroma of His glory can pour out and permeate our environment.

Our problem is that so many of us are all bottled up and sealed tight in jobs or circumstances or attitudes that restrict us. God can't "smell" our glory, so He applies a little pressure and breaks the seal. We want to cry out, "God, You're killing me!" He replies, "No, I just want to release your scent to the world. I want them to see what's inside you; the glory *I* put there."

> *In one way or another, God has to break our "jars of clay" in order for His fragrant glory to come out.*

Paul, the New Testament church leader and missionary, came to understand clearly from his own experience this crushing process of God. Looking back over his long years of ministry, Paul wrote to Timothy, his son in the faith,

For I am already being poured out like a drink offering, and the time has come for my departure. I have fought the good fight, I have finished the race, I have kept the faith. Now there is in store for me the crown of righteousness, which the Lord, the righteous Judge, will award to me on that day—and not only to me, but also to all who have longed for His appearing (2 Timothy 4:6-8).

Under the Jewish sacrificial system, a drink offering was poured on a sacrifice before the sacrifice was offered up to God. Paul was pressed and squeezed, bruised, broken, and crushed, but he had no regrets. All his travail and hardship had served to expose the glory inside. Paul's glory was to carry the gospel of Jesus Christ to every corner of the Roman Empire. He had completed that assignment and was ready to depart. Paul would die empty. He would not take his glory to the grave.

❖ The Glory of Living

Maybe you are going through troubles in your life right now. Perhaps you are thinking, *I've had more problems since I became a believer than I did before.* What's really happening is that God is starting to expose you. He's rubbing away the outer layers of the world to uncover the real you. He's crushing your life in order to break the jar that conceals His glory. His fragrance is seeping through the cracks and into the environment around you. Some will like the smell; many will not. Those who do will glorify God for what they see Him doing in you. Those who don't will attack you. For them, the smell of glory is the stench of death. Consider what Paul wrote to the church in Corinth:

> **But thanks be to God, who always leads us in triumphal procession in Christ and through us spreads everywhere the fragrance of the knowledge of Him. For we are to God the aroma of Christ among those who are being saved and those who are perishing. To the one we are the smell of death; to the other, the fragrance of life. And who is equal to such a task?** (2 Corinthians 2:14-16)

Have you ever thought of yourself as "the aroma of Christ" or "the fragrance of life"? Even if you've had little exposure in the past, if you want to tap into your hidden glory God will start revealing Himself through you. He wants you to be part of His plan to fill the earth with His glory. The more He exposes you, the more people around you will begin to say, "Wow! It smells like Heaven around here!" or "Do you smell that fragrance? The presence of God has been here!"

Seeing yourself as "the aroma of Christ" and "the fragrance of life" should change the way you approach your circumstances. That's why you can thank God for what you've been going through this past week or this past month. Don't be mad or upset with God any more over all the difficulties you faced last year. Instead, thank Him. Thank God for the glory He is bringing out of you. Thank Him for the privilege of exposing His glory. Thank Him for the revelation He has given you that allows you to understand your circumstances from

His perspective. Thank Him for the confidence and assurance He has given you that you can handle everything that you're going through. Thank Him for the promise that He will not place on you more than you can bear.

Coal subjected to great pressure turns to diamond. God's pressure will not destroy you; it will purify you. Gold is refined by fire as all its impurities are burned away. The last "impurity" to be removed is *silver*. If *pure* gold is your goal, then even silver is undesirable. God's refining furnace will not burn you up. It will only burn away the "impurities" of the world that are hiding your glory. When we surrender ourselves to God's refining process, He will crush whatever He needs to crush, burn away whatever He needs to burn away, and afflict whatever He needs to afflict in order to get rid of whatever is blocking our glory. God will do whatever He needs to do to get His glory out of us.

*H*ave you ever thought of yourself as "the aroma of Christ" or "the fragrance of life"?

Manifesting God's Glory

This whole issue of crushing reveals three secrets for manifesting the glory of God.

1. The glory of God is manifested when demands are made on our potential.

2. The glory of God is revealed when we work out our potential.

3. The glory of God is exposed through the challenges of life.

These three principles ought to encourage us for the rest of our lives. If we know and understand them, we should never have another "bad day." This is because they teach us to see our lives and our circumstances from God's perspective. God does everything with a view to His purpose and glory. No matter how "bad" our day may seem, it is a good day for the glory.

God's nature is manifested when demands are made on our lives. That's why we don't grow very much during good times. No demands are being made on our hidden glory. Demands on our potential focus our attention and challenge us to be at our best. Our Manufacturer designed us to be workers. Work thrives best in an atmosphere of challenge. Life's demands challenge our potential, and as we work out that potential, our hidden glory is exposed.

Challenge brings out God's glory. Pressure brings forth His purpose. Even though we may not like to think about it, affliction is part of God's glorification program for us. It is one of the ways He refines us and brings out His glory.

> **See, I have refined you, though not as silver; I have tested you in the furnace of affliction. For My own sake, for My own sake, I do this. How can I let Myself be defamed? I will not yield My glory to another** (Isaiah 48:10-11).

This is one of those verses we sometimes wish was not in the Bible. God *tests* us in the "furnace of affliction." Why? Is it because He is cruel and heartless? Is it because He is capricious and arbitrary? No. These are characteristics of the false gods that Israel's neighbors worshiped. God tests us to *refine* us, to purify us as gold. He tests us for His own sake, that is, for His reputation. God puts us through the fire in order to expose His glory.

Any manufacturer tests its products thoroughly before putting them on the market. Design, function, and performance are rigorously examined before the company's name goes on the product because the manufacturer's reputation is at stake. If the product fails to perform as advertised, the company's reputation and credibility will suffer. That's why each product comes with a warranty. The manufacturer says, "We want you to be satisfied. If our product fails to perform according to its design, or fails to meet your expectations, send it back to us. We take responsibility for our products."

God is the same way. He tests us to prove us and purify us and refine us and make sure we will "perform" according to His design; that we will display His glory. His "furnace of affliction" may be uncomfortable at the time, but we will come out better for it in the end. We will realize our full potential and God will be glorified.

As believers, we are God's children and He is very jealous for us and has our very best interests at heart. Like any loving parent, our Father disciplines us in order to bring us to maturity. David, the psalmist-king of Israel, wrote, "Many are the afflictions of the righteous, but the Lord delivers him out of them all" (Ps. 34:19 NAS). Have you ever heard it said of someone who weathered a difficult situation that he came through it "smelling like a rose"? That's what God wants for us. Life will crush, press, and afflict us, but God has His hand on us, and He will see to it that we come through the fire with our clothes smelling not of smoke but of the fragrance of glory.

Glory in the Furnace

The Old Testament Book of Daniel tells the story of three young Hebrew men who endured the furnace of affliction for the glory of God. After the Babylonian Empire conquered the nation of Judah in 586 B.C., many Jews were taken in captivity back to Babylon. Among them were three young men who were trained to serve in the royal palace of King Nebuchadnezzar. We know them today by their Babylonian names: Shadrach, Meshach, and Abednego. Although they served the Babylonian king faithfully and loyally, their first allegiance was to God.

Everything went well until the day Nebuchadnezzar erected a huge golden idol and ordered all the people to worship it. Any who refused would be thrown into a blazing furnace. Shadrach, Meshach, and Abednego remained faithful to God and refused to worship the idol. Furious with rage, Nebuchadnezzar summoned the three to him and gave them one more chance to comply with his order to worship his idol. Then he threw down the gauntlet:

"But if you do not worship it, you will be thrown immediately into a blazing furnace. Then what god will be able to rescue you from my hand?" (Dan. 3:15b)

The three young men rose to the challenge.

Shadrach, Meshach and Abednego replied to the king, "O Nebuchadnezzar, we do not need to defend ourselves before you in this matter. If we are thrown into the blazing furnace, the God we serve is able to save us from it, and He will rescue us from your hand, O king. But even if He does not, we want you to know, O king, that we will not serve your gods or worship the image of gold you have set up" (Daniel 3:16-18).

How's that for faith? They would rather die than disown God. Even a blazing furnace was preferable to idolatry.

Shadrach, Meshach, and Abednego were bound and then thrown into a furnace that had been heated to seven times its normal intensity, so hot that it killed the soldiers who threw them in. What happened next was certainly not what the angry king expected.

Then King Nebuchadnezzar leaped to his feet in amazement and asked his advisers, "Weren't there three men that we tied up and threw into the fire?" They replied, "Certainly, O king." He said, "Look! I see four men walking around in the fire, unbound and unharmed, and the fourth looks like a son of the gods." Nebuchadnezzar then approached the opening of the blazing furnace and shouted, "Shadrach, Meshach and Abednego, servants of the Most High God, come out! Come here!" So Shadrach, Meshach and Abednego came out of the fire, and the satraps, prefects, governors and royal advisers crowded around them. They saw that the fire had not harmed their bodies, nor was a hair of their heads singed; their robes were not scorched, and there was no smell of fire on them. Then Nebuchadnezzar said, "Praise be to the God

of Shadrach, Meshach and Abednego, who has sent His angel and rescued His servants! They trusted in Him and defied the king's command and were willing to give up their lives rather than serve or worship any god except their own God" (Daniel 3:24-28).

Shadrach, Meshach, and Abednego went through the "furnace of affliction" and came out "smelling like a rose." God honored their faithfulness and delivered them safely through the fire. This experience refined them and prepared them for greater work. If their faith was strong *before* the fiery furnace, imagine how strong it must have been *afterward*! God accomplished a broader purpose here as well: His name was glorified before a pagan king and his advisers. Nebuchadnezzar witnessed the glory and power of the true God manifested in and through the lives of Shadrach, Meshach, and Abednego. As a result, the king was moved to call them "servants of the Most High God," and to exclaim, "Praise be to the God of Shadrach, Meshach, and Abednego!" Then he promoted them to higher positions of responsibility and honor.

God allowed His servants to go through the fire so a pagan king could come to know Him. Those servants were willing to be afflicted in order for God to be glorified. The circumstances of life "crushed" Shadrach, Meshach, and Abednego, and they emerged redolent with the fragrance of glory.

Growth Is Glory Exposed

None of us knows who we really are until trouble comes. God takes us through tough times and difficult challenges in order to show the rest of the world what He has put inside us. He wants to bring out some of His nature in us; to apply the pressure so that when we come out shining, people say to us, "I didn't know you were that strong. How did you make it? It must be God." Whether or not they realize it, they smell the sweet fragrance of glory that God has squeezed out of us.

❖ The Glory of Living

The crushing press of life and the furnace of affliction bring growth and maturity in our lives. Growth is glory exposed, putting on full display that which is hidden inside. Maturity is the full flowering of the seed, the full exercise of potential. Maturity for an apple seed is an apple tree, but the seed must be "crushed" before the tree will come forth.

Have you ever been through a particularly difficult or challenging situation and afterward said something like, "That stretched me," or "I've grown because of that"? What you mean is that you handled something you never would have believed you could handle. Now it's a part of your life and your experience and you are better and more mature as a result. The pressure of the circumstances brought qualities out of you that you didn't even know you had. What we call growth God calls glory exposure.

No matter who we are or what we have accomplished, we all have glory inside that still needs to come out, and God is determined to see us release it. As long as we follow our own initiative, God doesn't have to act. Sometimes, however, there are God-sized things that He wants to expose in us; things that we are *afraid* to do, don't believe we *can* do, or simply don't *want* to do. That's when God acts to give us some incentive. Life suddenly shifts a little on us, adversity blindsides us, and God says, "This is to bring out some of the stuff you don't even know is there." We reach the other side and all at once it dawns on us that not only did we make it, but we don't even smell like smoke.

Maturity is the goal of life and growth is the key. Without growth there *is* no life. If we are not growing, we are dying. Whether it comes sooner or later, the result is the same. Whatever God allows us to go through is for our good, to bring us to maturity and expose our glory. From now on we should never ask God, "Why me?" Instead, we should say, "Use me." We should say, "Bring out Your glory through this situation, and teach me what You want me to learn from it so I can grow. Lead me into maturity and show me how to use this circumstance to bring out my full potential."

Reclaiming Our Glory

Jesus Christ's purpose in coming to earth in the flesh was to secure, reclaim, and manifest the glory that is inside every human being. At the very beginning of His public ministry, Jesus taught concerning the characteristics of that glory. Matthew recorded the words of Jesus' first public sermon in his Gospel:

What we call growth God calls glory exposure.

> **Blessed are the poor in spirit, for theirs is the kingdom of heaven. Blessed are those who mourn, for they will be comforted. Blessed are the meek, for they will inherit the earth. Blessed are those who hunger and thirst for righteousness, for they will be filled. Blessed are the merciful, for they will be shown mercy. Blessed are the pure in heart, for they will see God. Blessed are the peacemakers, for they will be called sons of God. Blessed are those who are persecuted because of righteousness, for theirs is the kingdom of heaven** (Matthew 5:3-10).

These words paint a vivid picture of the nature and character of people who have the right attitude and perspective toward God, themselves, and their fellowmen. They are people who live daily with their glory exposed, blessed of God and being a blessing to everyone they meet. As they pass through the earth they leave an unmistakable "glory fragrance" wherever they go.

After these "beatitudes," Jesus zeroes in and makes everything more personal, climaxing the introduction to His sermon with these words:

> **You are the light of the world. A city on a hill cannot be hidden. Neither do people light a lamp and put it under a bowl. Instead they put it on its stand, and it gives light to everyone in the house. In the same way, let your light shine before men, that they may see your good deeds and praise your Father in heaven** (Matthew 5:14-16).

Our assignment on earth as humans is not to be timid or apologetic, but bold with our vision, powerful with our dreams, diligent in pursuing our ideas, and passionate in our work. God never does anything halfheartedly or without purpose, and neither should we. We should live and work with passion and purpose because that is the nature of God, and He created us to be like Him. Our goal should be that people would see us and look to God.

We cannot reclaim our glory or reach our full potential outside of a personal love relationship with Jesus Christ. Jesus said, "I am the way and the truth and the life. No one comes to the Father except through Me" (Jn. 14:6). The only way we can reenter "Eden," the covering environment of the Father's presence, is through the doorway of Jesus Christ. Until then, the best we can hope for is to be a dim shadow of what God wants for us. We were created for His presence, and apart from His presence we will never become all He wants us to be. Apart from the presence of God we will never expose our "full weight." Only in Christ can we reclaim and manifest our full glory.

Let Your Life Reveal Your Glory

What is God's purpose for your life? What vision has He given you? These are important questions because God has appointed you to a unique assignment. God has chosen you to live a life of glory for Him that no one else on earth can live. If you don't already know, ask Him to reveal to you His purpose and vision for your life. You are filled with untapped glory. God did not give it to you by accident. He put you here on earth to release your glory. Let your life reveal your glory.

Your purpose and vision are your glory. God gave them to *you*, not to somebody else. Only you can fulfill your purpose or realize your vision. No one else can. You are a "jar of clay" with God's precious glory stored inside. He endowed you with gifts and talents to use in living out your purpose. *Your gifts and talents were given to you in order to release your glory.* Don't bury them away as the wicked and unfaithful servant did in Jesus' parable (see Matt. 25:14-30). Don't die in seed form. True success in life is to die empty, with everything you are poured out completely until nothing is left.

The world needs your glory. Does that statement surprise you? So many of us have come to believe that we have little or nothing to offer in life. That idea is a lie from the devil. Each of us is part of God's master plan for creation. You have something the world needs that no one but you can give. Don't die with your glory still inside. Don't take your glory to the grave. *The earth is waiting for your glory.*

Paul understood this. In his letter to the church in Rome he writes:

> **Now if we are children, then we are heirs—heirs of God and co-heirs with Christ, if indeed we share in His sufferings in order that we may also share in His glory. I consider that our present sufferings are not worth comparing with the glory that will be revealed in us. The creation waits in eager expectation for the sons of God to be revealed. For the creation was subjected to frustration, not by its own choice, but by the will of the one who subjected it, in hope that the creation itself will be liberated from its bondage to decay and brought into the glorious freedom of the children of God** (Romans 8:17-21).

If you are a believer, you are part of God's plan to free all of creation from the bondage and decay that sin has caused. If you are not a believer, then you are one of those who need to be set free. Christ is the one who sets us free, and in Him we can fulfill the purpose of God for our lives.

What is God's purpose for your life? While the specific assignment will be unique to you, the general purpose is the same. Whatever your unique vision, whatever your gifts and talents, this is God's purpose for your life:

Leave your glory on earth before you die.

❖ The Glory of Living

Let God break your "jar of clay" and pour you out like precious perfume that will leave a heavenly fragrance behind after you have gone. Live your life to its fullest for the glory of God. Don't be afraid to take some risks, to try new things, to confront new challenges. You will never really know what's inside you until you face a situation that is bigger than you are. That's when God can go to work and "do immeasurably more than all we ask or imagine, according to His power that is at work within us" (Eph. 3:20).

Like the Olympic torchbearer, "let your light shine before men, that they may see your good deeds and praise your Father in heaven" (Matt. 5:16). If we are faithful in this, we will hasten the day when God's promise will come to pass:

For the earth will be filled with the knowledge of the glory of the Lord, as the waters cover the sea (Habakkuk 2:14).

❖ PRINCIPLES ❖

1. Our glory exists not for our own benefit but for others.

2. The glory of God is manifested when demands are made on our potential.

3. The glory of God is revealed when we work out our potential.

4. The glory of God is exposed through the challenges of life.

5. Growth is glory exposed.

6. Your purpose and vision are your glory.

7. Your gifts and talents were given to you in order to release your glory.

8. The world needs your glory.

9. The earth is waiting for your glory.

10. Leave your glory on earth before you die.

The Glory
of Living
Study Guide

Contents

How to Use this G L O R Y Study Guide. . . . 181

Chapter One   The Nature of Glory. 183

Chapter Two   The Environment of Glory. 191

Chapter Three   Glory in an "Earth Suit" 199

Chapter Four   The Glory of "Becoming". 207

Chapter Five   The Presence and the Glory 215

Chapter Six   Restoring the Environment of Glory. 223

Chapter Seven   Squeezing the Glory Out 231

Chapter Eight   Jesus—Revealing God's Glory 239

Chapter Nine   Releasing the Glory. 247

Chapter Ten   The Fragrance of Glory 257

How to Use this GLORY Study Guide

This study guide is a companion to *The Glory of Living* by Dr. Myles Munroe. The lessons are designed to be used privately or in an intimate group setting. Adapt liberally to suit your needs. Pages from the book by Myles Munroe are listed for easy reference.

God's glory is widely misunderstood by many people, even Christians. We tend to think it is a shining light that surrounds God's throne and has little to do with us. Dr. Munroe makes it quite clear in his book that we are not casually involved in God's glory but are key to its very manifestation. The lessons in this study guide, therefore, are designed to involve the reader in the concepts of the book. Questions are distributed between ones that target the mind, ones that target the heart, and ones that target the will.

Take time with each lesson to participate with the concepts. The word **GLORY** is used as an acrostic to guide your attention to the following:

Gain insights through challenging your mind and paradigms.

Look it up. Be confident in what the Word of God says and how it applies to you.

Order your thoughts. It's decision time to determine what you believe in your heart.

Rehearse your plan to change. Action steps put feet to what you've learned.

Your next step to glory. This involves meditation, prayer, and worship, using the concepts offered in the book.

To make Dr. Munroe's book be most effective will require a change in your life. Change is always preceded by hard work, so roll up your sleeves and have at it!

The Glory of Living
Study Guide

Chapter One

The Nature of Glory

"Glory is the full expression of God's nature" (p. 18).

All created things declare God's glory by their very existence, except for one. Man is the only creation who can choose to declare God's glory or not.

In your own words, write a paragraph from your understanding of Chapter One that contrasts the glory that shines from creation and the glory that shines from human beings.

_____

_____

_____

_____

Where have you seen God's glory rest "heavy" or "weighty?" (see p. 18)

_____

_____

1

G
L
O
R
Y

Gain
Perspective

Kabod—
"fullness"
"full weight"
"glory"

G
L
O
R
Y

Gain
Perspective

continued

Dr. Munroe speaks about God's "self-disclosure." How does God self-disclose? In what ways have you seen this?

_____

_____

_____

_____

_____

_____

Since Jesus gives us the best picture of God's glory, write ten ways in which you think He did this (see p. 19).

1. _____

2. _____

3. _____

4. _____

5. _____

6. _____

7. _____

8. _____

9. _____

10. _____

2

G
L
O
R
Y

Look
It Up

"The heavens
declare the
glory of
God…"
Ps. 19:1

Dr. Munroe tells us that the glory of God is the full nature of God on display (see p. 20). Read Romans 1:20. What does this tell us about the witness of nature to God's existence? What are your favorite ways that God displays His glory in nature?

_____

_____

Read Psalm 29:1-2. Reread the verses, inserting your name after "O mighty ones." How can you ascribe to God Almighty anything of value?

_____

_____

Look up Isaiah 6:3b. Write your own psalm of glory using this verse as a response between each of your lines. We have started your psalm below:
God's glory is seen as the day begins and ends.
Holy, holy, holy is the Lord Almighty; the whole earth is full of His glory.
I see His splendor as each rainbow paints the sky.
Holy, holy, holy is the Lord Almighty; the whole earth is
   full of His glory.
Etc.

_____

_____

Read Genesis 1:26-28. What is man's unique job description? (see p. 23)

_____

_____

3

G
L
O
R
Y

Order
Your
Thoughts

God has put
Himself on
display

What does the weight of God's person and reputation mean to you? (see p. 19)

_____

_____

Is it that God's glory is contagious as a disease…or is it that God's DNA is in everything He touches? Explain your opinion (see p. 21).

_____

_____

_____

What are the four things needed for a creature to fully display its glory? (see pp. 21-22) Which of these four are totally dependent upon God?

_____

_____

_____

"Man is His [God's] masterpiece" (p. 23). What palette of colors did God use to create you, His masterpiece? Why?

_____

_____

_____

How well does your life put God's glory on exhibition? What might you do to increase your exhibit? (see p. 19)

_____

_____

_____

_____

Dr. Munroe says, "God is pleased when His creations manifest their glory—and His—by becoming everything He created them to be" (p. 22). What has God created you to be? Are you growing into that creation? What are your plans to continue growing in that direction?

_____

_____

"…then the glory of man is to *be* like God and to *rule* like God in fellowship and harmony *with* God" (p. 24). How well are you doing this? What might you do to better fulfill this call?

_____

_____

How can you purpose to be in a state of worship all the time? (see p. 27) List some things you must change for this to be able to happen.

_____

_____

4

G
L
O
R
Y

Rehearse Your Plan to Change

"…characteristic qualities of His nature… best seen through… the lives of believers"

5

G
L
O
R
Y

Your Next
Step to Glory

"God alone is
the 'guilty'
party. He
alone is
responsible
for creation."

Spend some time "blaming" God for his great works (see p. 20).

_____

_____

_____

"Whatever our Daddy got, we got" (p. 25). Reflect on what "you got" from your Daddy. Thank Him profusely for each blessing.

_____

_____

_____

You are the spitting image of God (see p. 25). Can a "critic" see through your forgery or are you the genuine article? Ask the Lord to forgive you for the ways in which you forge a fake lifestyle.

_____

_____

_____

Commit to "exposing" God's glory today (see p. 26). Let God dig down through your junk to let His glory out.

_____

_____

_____

SUMMARY

Reread the principles on page 28. As you do, reflect on each statement by what you have learned, how you need to change, your plan to accomplish the goal of change, the results of your actions. Journal your experiences as you proceed with this **GLORY** study guide.

G

L

O

R

Y

_____

_____

_____

_____

_____

_____

_____

_____

_____

_____

_____

_____

Chapter Two

The Environment of Glory

"The only way we can really learn how to be like God and to rule like God is to live in an environment that is permeated with the presence of God" (p. 30).

Dr. Munroe says that we are "to live in an environment that is permeated with the presence of God" (p. 30). In your own words, describe this.

_____

_____

_____

Describe your "garden of delight" (Eden). What would it contain physically, emotionally, and spiritually? (see p. 32)

_____

_____

_____

_____

1

G
L
O
R
Y

Gain
Perspective

Eden, from a primitive root *adan*, which means "soft," or "pleasant"

G
L
O
R
Y

Gain
Perspective

continued

"Eden was more an environment than a location" (p. 32). In your opinion, what does this mean?

_____

_____

Why do you think Western philosophies do not embrace the idea that the freedom to choose disproves the theory of evolution? (see p. 36)

_____

_____

Dr. Munroe states that purity is related to transparency. Where do you find it easy to be transparent and where don't you?

_____

_____

Do you think Adam saw his eviction from Eden as an act of God's mercy? Would you have? (see p. 42)

_____

_____

Can you be a believer and still be a restless wanderer like Cain? Why or why not? (see p. 43)

_____

_____

Look up Exodus 34:29-35. The presence of God was very evident on Moses. Describe when you have sensed the presence of God (see p. 34).

_____

_____

_____

Read Philippians 3:20. Contrast and compare your citizenship to your country to your citizenship in Heaven (see p. 38).

_____

_____

_____

Look at First Peter 1:4. It says that we have a spiritual inheritance. What do we inherit? (see p. 38)

_____

_____

_____

Read Revelation 21:3b about the new earth. What will be new? (see p. 38)

_____

_____

_____

2

G
L
O
R
Y

Look
It Up

"The highest heavens belong to the Lord, but the earth He has given to man."
Ps. 115:16

3

G
L
O
R
Y

**Order
Your
Thoughts**

"Without
the Holy
Spirit, man
can never
experience
his full glory."

Dr. Munroe tells us that as long as Adam remained in the Garden, he experienced perfect joy and complete fulfillment. How can you remain in the Garden God has planned for you?

_____

_____

_____

Genesis 1:28 speaks of man multiplying and replenishing the earth. How have you reproduced (multiplied)? What of God have you duplicated? (see p. 33)

_____

_____

_____

In your own words, describe the difference between the presence of God and the glory of God (see p. 34).

_____

_____

_____

Why is the Holy Spirit so important to you personally? (see p. 42)

_____

_____

_____

Dr. Munroe points out that Adam and Eve fellow-shiped continuously with God (see p. 35). How can you move toward this?

_____

_____

"True freedom always comes with limits and obedience is meaningful only where standards of behavior exist" (p. 36). Explain this in your own words. What limits do you challenge? How can you not just accept those limits but embrace them?

_____

_____

_____

On page 37 of *The Glory of Living*, we read of Adam and Eve after the Fall, "The rulers became refugees." What steps do you need to take to progress from refugee to ruler?

_____

_____

_____

Do you see your future as "undisplayed glory"? (see p. 40) Are you ready to prepare yourself for such a future?

_____

_____

4

G
L
O
R
Y

Rehearse
Your Plan
to Change

"Without
God's pres-
ence, man
has no
purpose,
life is an
experiment."

5

G
L
O
R
Y

**Your Next
Step to Glory**

"Our will
has become
a victim of
our fallen,
corrupt
nature."

On pages 37-40, Dr. Munroe lists six things that man did not lose in the Fall. List these and rehearse them to your soul. Thank God for each one.

_____

_____

_____

_____

Describe the three parts of your soul (see p. 39). What steps will you take this week to make these three conform to the image of Christ?

_____

_____

_____

Reread # 1 on pages 40-41. Pray for purity in your life. Meditate on God's holiness and let Him transform you. Pray that integrity would mark everything you do.

_____

_____

"Protecting God's presence should be our priority" (p. 45). How can you do this? Pray that you will begin today to protect God's glory.

_____

_____

SUMMARY

Reread the nine principles on page 47. As you do, read them out loud and use the personal pronouns "I" or "me" where it uses "we" or "man." Write these below. Journal your experiences as you proceed with this **GLORY** study guide.

_____

_____

_____

_____

_____

_____

_____

_____

_____

_____

_____

_____

_____

_____

G

L

O

R

Y

The Glory of Living
Study Guide

Chapter Three

Glory in an "Earth Suit"

"Will your glory ever be on display for others to enjoy?" (p. 50)

List the benefits you utilize from other people's glory just during the period of time from when you awake until you eat breakfast (see p. 49).

_____

_____

_____

_____

Dr. Munroe tells us "[the] ignorance of our identity and purpose as humans pervades every society and culture around the world" (p. 50). How many people do you know who are ignorant of their identity and purpose?

_____

_____

_____

1

G
L
O
R
Y

Gain
Perspective

"Glory is tangible"

G
L
O
R
Y

Gain
Perspective

continued

"[God] imparted to us some of His nature, His character, and His attributes" (p. 52). What of these three do you have?

_____

_____

How do you think the Fall has affected us as carriers of God's glory? How hasn't it affected us? (see p. 53)

_____

_____

"God did not create us to make a living, but to show the world what He is like" (p. 62). How does your career fit in with your mandate to be an expression of God's glory? How can you use it better?

_____

_____

Why is it necessary for God's glory to be seen in the Church? See Ephesians 3:20-21 (p. 62).

_____

_____

Are all people creative? Support your answer with your personal observations. How can more glory come out of us? (see p. 62)

_____

_____

Read First Samuel 13:14 and Acts 13:22. David was a man after God's own heart. What do you think that means? (see p. 51)

_____

_____

Reread Psalm 8:1,3-8 (NAS version, if possible), putting your name in place of "man" or "him." Pull out statements of your status in regards to other creation (see p. 51).

_____

_____

_____

Look at Deuteronomy 32:19-21a. Why does our turning away from God cause Him to turn His face from us? (see p. 54)

_____

_____

Read Isaiah 42:5-9. In your own words, explain the context and meaning of this passage. What have you learned by reading Dr. Munroe's thoughts on these verses? (see p. 57)

_____

_____

_____

2

G
L
O
R
Y

Look
It Up

"...they exchanged their Glory for an image of a bull..."
Ps. 106:20

3

G
L
O
R
Y

Order
Your
Thoughts

God has put
Himself on
display

Dr. Munroe says we exchange our royal heritage for self-pity and guilt (see p. 50). Do you operate as if you are royalty? Do you wallow in guilt and self-pity? Why or why not?

_____

_____

_____

Concerning man, Dr. Munroe writes, "…humanity's apparent smallness against the backdrop of Creation…" "…You have made him (man) a little lower than God…" (see p. 52). In your own words, explain these seemingly opposing facts.

_____

_____

If you are "crowned" with "glory and majesty," how will people see these in you as you live out your day? (see p. 52)

_____

_____

Explain your typical reaction to someone who compliments you on a gift or talent. Are you operating in the way that God desires? (see p. 56)

_____

_____

_____

Dr. Munroe writes, "My question to you is…will your glory ever be on display for others to enjoy?" (p. 50) Meditate on this question. Jot down some thoughts in the space below.

_____

_____

_____

Do you find you bow yourself to circumstances, relegating power to things that "just happen" to control your day, rather than recognizing God's sovereign hand in action? (see p. 54) What should you do to change this?

_____

_____

In your own words, define humility. How do you exercise it? What steps do you need to take to exercise it in a greater fashion? (see p. 55)

_____

_____

How are you currently using God's treasure? In what way can you use it to a greater degree? (see p. 60)

_____

_____

_____

4

G
L
O
R
Y

Rehearse
Your Plan
to Change

"God hid
His 'treasure'
inside our
'jars of
clay'…"

5

G
L
O
R
Y

Your Next
Step to Glory

"God alone is
the 'guilty'
party. He
alone is
responsible
for creation."

Dr. Munroe tells us to "give credit to God" (p. 56). Take some time right now to credit God with all the glory He has placed in you.

_____

_____

"We were made to be masters of our environment, not slaves of it" (p. 58). Translate this statement to your own life. Where do you feel more like a slave than a master? Confess to the Lord how you have given more glory (authority, power) to that which enslaves you. Speak over that issue, "I will not give glory to another!" Ask the Holy Spirit to remind you not to fall into the same trap again.

_____

_____

_____

Of what are you fearful or intimidated? Begin with any areas in your life where you feel discouragement, or have a bad attitude, or seem to get negative thoughts or opinions. Renounce each one. Declare boldly what you have in Jesus. As each item is swept away, deposit "goblets of glory" in your mind and heart (see p. 59).

_____

_____

_____

_____

SUMMARY

Reread the 12 principles on pages 63-64. Highlight one key word from each statement. Say these twelve words out loud three times. In your own words, explain each word. Journal your experiences as you proceed with this **GLORY** study guide.

G
L
O
R
Y

_____

_____

_____

_____

_____

_____

_____

_____

_____

_____

_____

_____

_____

_____

The Glory of Living
Study Guide

Chapter Four

The Glory of "Becoming"

"Godly success is fully exposing the glory within us" (p. 69).

What of your potential lies on a "garbage heap"? (p. 66) Why?

_____

_____

Define "godly success" (p. 68) in your own words. What does it mean in your life today?

_____

_____

Dr. Munroe tells us that we are to "work" and "take care of" our environment (see p. 69). At what has God commissioned you to work? And what has He commissioned you to "take care of" in this world?

_____

_____

_____

1

G
L
O
R
Y

Gain
Perspective

"Godly success... focuses not on the outward but on the inward."

G
L
O
R
Y

Gain
Perspective

continued

Explain how death and glory are related (see p. 78). Give an example of how glory came out of death in your own life.

_____

_____

God's Word tells us to "be perfect" (see Matt. 5:48). How are you perfect...right now? (see pp. 76-77)

_____

_____

When God says "well done," how do you know it? (see p. 78) Do you hear God speak these words to you? In what way?

_____

_____

_____

_____

Dr. Munroe states, "Our purpose in life is to get rid of our glory. Life is about glory manifestations" (p. 79). If this is the case, how does one prevent oneself from being used up?

_____

_____

_____

Read Jeremiah 29:10-14. Do you really believe verse 11? Read this passage again, inserting your name throughout. Think through your life. Out of what has God brought you? Through what is He presently bringing you? Where will He lead you from here? (see p. 68)

_____

_____

_____

Do you ever feel like you are searching "vainly" in your career, relationships, or ministry? How do you cling to your Creator at a time like this? (see p. 73)

_____

_____

Look up Ecclesiastes 9:10a and Colossians 3:23-24. Rewrite these verses, including specific situations or issues about your job, a ministry, or relationship. (Ex.: "Whatever you do, Jan, teaching piano...") (See page 77.)

_____

_____

Read First Peter 1:15-16. How holy are you? Do you know how to tap into the potential of holiness? (see p. 80)

_____

_____

2

G
L
O
R
Y

Look
It Up

"You will seek
Me
and find
Me when
you seek Me
with all your
heart."
Jer. 29:13

3

Order
Your
Thoughts

"Our roles
may all be dif-
ferent,
but our
purpose is
the same: to
glorify God."

How does your environment have to change to be more Edenic? (see p. 69) What can you do to "help things along"? How do you need to pray?

_____

_____

"As man is the image and glory of God, his work is the expression and exposure of God's glory and nature" (p. 70). Do you feel this way about the job you currently work? Why or why not?

_____

_____

Dr. Munroe gives an analogy of seeds and God's glory (pp. 73-75). What seed is in you? What is the planting stage for you? The sprouting stage? The blossoming stage? The fruit-bearing stage?

_____

_____

_____

What are you becoming? Do you like the seeds of glory within you? Are you ready to produce healthy growth? (see p. 75)

_____

_____

_____

So that you might have "no regrets," what dread or doubts do you need to dispel? What hope do you need to put feet to this week? (see p. 67)

_____

_____

Where do lethargy, laziness, or procrastination enter your life? How can you dispose of these and push forward? (see p. 79)

_____

_____

_____

Where do you need to rise above your earthly environment? What do you need to do to create a heavenly environment within the earthly one? (see p. 81)

_____

_____

_____

"The 'glory of becoming' is discovering what we were born to do, putting our hand diligently to that work for the glory of God..." (p. 81). Describe your diligence quotient.

_____

_____

_____

4

G
L
O
R
Y

Rehearse Your Plan to Change

"...one definition of glory is the full expression of the true nature of a thing."

211 ❖

5

G
L
O
R
Y

Your Next
Step to Glory

"God
programmed
growth and
maturity
into every
living thing
He created."

If you are dissatisfied in your career or your ministry, whether in part or whole, find a good counselor to identify why you are dissatisfied and what you need to do to redeem your work or ministry (p. 71).

_____

_____

Take time to praise God for the following: dreams, ideas, passions, imagination, creativity, and hope. Pray that the environment in which you live will be right for the above to flourish (p. 75).

_____

_____

"Hang out" with God right now. Worship Him and let His glory come out (p. 76).

_____

_____

Take some time to confess your sin to the Lord. Confess those things that keep your holiness from finding its place in you (p. 81).

_____

_____

_____

_____

SUMMARY?

Reread the 12 principles on pages 83-84. Renumber them in order of importance as you look at your own life. Use them as a check to see where you are. Journal your experiences as you poceed with this **GLORY** study guide.

_____

_____

_____

_____

_____

_____

_____

_____

_____

_____

_____

_____

_____

_____

_____

_____

_____

G

L

O

R

Y

The Glory of Living
Study Guide

Chapter Five

The Presence and the Glory

"Walking with God under the covering shelter of His presence should be our day-by-day, moment-by-moment experience" (pp. 86-87).

Dr. Munroe writes, "Mankind lost the presence of God at the Fall, but most of us act as though we don't even miss it" (p. 86). On a scale of one to ten, how badly do you miss the presence of God when it is not around you? Explain your answer.

_____

_____

_____

We are not to presume upon God, for this brings defeat (see p. 89). How does one presume upon God? Is there any presumption on your part?

_____

_____

_____

_____

1

G
L
O
R
Y

Gain
Perspective

"God's presence is a prerequisite for relation-ship with Him."

G
L
O
R
Y

Gain
Perspective

continued

"He wants to reveal His glory in us and help us reach our full potential, but He will not force it on us" (p. 90). Where does your free will conflict with the opportunity to reveal God's glory within you?

_____

_____

On page 91, read the paragraph under the heading **God's Presence Versus God's Glory**. Write a three-word definition for God's presence and a three-word definition for God's glory, based on Dr. Munroe's words.

_____

_____

We need to distinguish between God's omnipresence and His manifest presence (pp. 91-92). What does this mean to you? Give an example of a time when you have seen God's manifest presence by experience and another when you knew God's omnipresence by faith.

_____

_____

_____

Dr. Munroe outlines the word glory on page 93. Define glory in your own words. When have you seen God's glory?

_____

_____

Take the last sentence on page 93 and fill in the equations below.

God's omnipresence   = know God's _____

God's manifest presence = know God's _____

God's glory   = know God's _____

G
L
O
R
Y

Gain
Perspective

continued

Read Psalm 139:7-12. Outlined here are sharp contrasts of where one might go to flee from God's presence. Write these below (see p. 92).

_____

_____

_____

Look up Psalm 34:1 (KJV). Based on this verse, why do you think praise is the ideal environment for man and creation? (see p. 95)

_____

_____

Read Psalm 22:3 (KJV). What does the word inhabitest mean to you? How much of your life excludes praise? How much of it exudes praise? (see p. 96)

_____

_____

_____

2

G
L
O
R
Y

Look
It Up

"The heavens declare the glory of God..."
Ps. 19:1

G
L
O
R
Y

**Look
It Up**

continued

Based on Matthew 5:16, tell how letting your light shine exposes the glory within you (see p. 96).

_____

_____

_____

_____

_____

_____

3

G
L
O
R
Y

**Order
Your
Thoughts**

"Glory is the open display of His attributes and character."

Dr. Munroe believes that our hearts do not expect a great move of God. Is this true in your experience? Why or why not? (p. 86)

_____

_____

_____

Dr. Munroe writes, "It is not normal for believers to go through life with no sense of God's presence or power" (p. 86). How normal is it for you to go through one day without the sense of God's presence?

_____

_____

_____

Where in your life do you feel the "energizing power of God"? (p. 89)

_____

_____

Where are you experiencing "spiritual laziness"? Where might you find "lack of discipline"? What does this mean to realizing your full potential? (p. 90)

_____

_____

_____

G
L
O
R
Y

Order
Your
Thoughts

continued

Take stock of your God-given talents, your relationships, and your ministry. Where has God's glory departed? What do you need in order to regain God's presence? (see p. 88)

_____

_____

_____

The choices are obedience and the presence, or disobedience and "ichabod" (see p. 90). What needs to change within you in order for you to choose obedience at the threshold of each temptation?

_____

_____

_____

4
G
L
O
R
Y

Rehearse
Your Plan
to Change

"God's
presence is
all-pervasive
but invisible.
His glory...is
tangible and
observable."

**G
L
O
R
Y**

**Rehearse
Your Plan
to Change**

continued

Name people to whom you have difficulty showing God's grace and mercy. Plan to show it this day. What will be your responses toward them? How will you appropriate the love of God and His glory? (see p. 91)

_____

_____

_____

"The critical factor is the attitude" (p. 97). How is your attitude in need of alignment to God's best? What are you going to do about it?

_____

_____

_____

**5
G
L
O
R
Y**

**Your Next
Step to Glory**

"Praise is the ideal environment for man and creation."

Examine your heart for unconfessed sin that lies within you that might stop you from sensing the presence of God (see p. 92).

_____

_____

_____

_____

_____

_____

Experience God's cleansing. Let Him change your unholiness to holiness, your unrighteousness to righteousness (see p. 96).

_____

_____

_____

_____

"Praise attracts God's presence" (p. 89). Take time to praise God right now. Attract God's presence. Sense His presence before you move on to other things.

_____

_____

_____

As you invite God to manifest His presence to you, give Him the freedom to reveal Himself in any way He chooses (see p. 93).

_____

_____

_____

_____

G
L
O
R
Y

Your Next Step to Glory

continued

G
L
O
R
Y

SUMMARY

Reread the 11 principles on page 98. Highlight the word presence in each sentence. How much do you practice the presence of God? Journal your experiences as you proceed with this **GLORY** study guide.

_____

_____

_____

_____

_____

_____

_____

_____

_____

_____

_____

_____

_____

_____

_____

_____

_____

_____

_____

Chapter Six

Restoring the Environment of Glory

"The presence of God is the ideal environment for man's glory" (p. 99).

Explain the Holy Spirit's role in creating an environment of praise (see p. 101).

_____

_____

"True praise is an exercise..." (p. 102). Make a comparison between praise and an exercise (ex.: aerobics).

_____

_____

Why is God worthy to be trusted? Is your answer from your head or your heart? (see p. 103)

_____

_____

_____

1

G
L
O
R
Y

Gain
Perspective

"The praise of our lips... re-creates the spiritual environment of Eden."

G
L
O
R
Y

Gain
Perspective

continued

How can praise reverse sin's effect? How does its positive force affect the negative? (see p. 103)

_____

_____

_____

How can praise become ritualistic? Do you ever day-dream in corporate worship? Has it become ritualis-tic in any way to you? (see p. 105)

_____

_____

_____

_____

List some ways to praise God. List some personal experiences you have had while worshiping God (see p. 109).

_____

_____

_____

_____

How does one prepare to "ascend the hill of the Lord"? (p. 105)

_____

_____

Look at Hebrews 13:15. What does "sacrifice of praise" mean to you? What do you personally sacrifice in praise? (see p. 101)

_____

_____

_____

Read John 15:5. What does abiding in Christ entail for you? (see p. 101)

_____

_____

Based on James 4:7-10, why do you believe humility is key to attracting God's presence? According to Dr. Munroe, what are the two results of our approaching God with a humble spirit? (see p. 102)

_____

_____

_____

Look at the story of Paul and Silas in Acts 16:25-26. Why do you think their praise caused such a violent response? What "chains" do you need loosed today? (see p. 108)

_____

_____

_____

2

G
L
O
R
Y

Look
It Up

"worship:
proskuneo,
literally
means 'to
kiss, like a
dog licking
his master's
hand'..."

3

G
L
O
R
Y

Order
Your
Thoughts

God has put
Himself on
display

Examine your praise life. Is there an atmosphere of praise that prevails over most of your day? Is Eden a possibility in your life? Explain (see p. 100).

_____

_____

"Our spirits...long to return...to that bright, vibrant, and vital relationship with God" (p. 100). Does this describe your current relationship with God? Have you had a time in the past when it did describe your relationship with Him? What were the ingredients that propagated such a relationship?

_____

_____

_____

In your situation, evaluate what is necessary for you to come before God in true worship. How are you able to become intimate with God? (see p. 110)

_____

_____

Think through your day. What must you order differently so that more praise might take place in your schedule? (see p. 111)

_____

_____

_____

Dr. Munroe tells us that the earth is filled with the consequences of our sin (see p. 100). How have you polluted your environment with your sin? What steps must you take in order to cleanse those pollutants?

_____

_____

In Genesis 3:1b, satan asked Eve, "Did God really say...?" Our response must be "YES! God REALLY said it!" Rehearse this over in your mind and heart for the times today when satan will ask you the same question (see p. 102).

_____

_____

"The inhabitants of Heaven praise God with undiluted and undivided devotion" (p. 104). What do you personally need to do to become undiluted and undivided in your devotion to God?

_____

_____

Think about a current situation or relationship that needs a shout or a battle cry to praise God's presence into it (see p. 107).

_____

_____

_____

4

G
L
O
R
Y

Rehearse
Your Plan
to Change

"...character-
istic qualities
of His
nature...
best seen
through...
the lives of
believers"

5

G
L
O
R
Y

Your Next
Step to Glory

"Praise is
something
we can do
anytime,
anywhere."

Take some time to "brag on" God. Time how long it takes before you run out of things to say (see p. 101).

_____

_____

Praise God's presence into the place where you are right now. Lift His name up and watch what happens! (see p. 106)

_____

_____

Page 104 cites three Scripture passages that include songs. Worship with these songs (with or without a melody). Sing or speak them into your environment.

_____

_____

_____

Become an "island of Eden" today (p. 101). Pray through the struggles you face before they even happen. Praise God until you sense a breakthrough. Take this island with you throughout the day.

_____

_____

SUMMARY

Reread the 12 principles on page 112. After each principle, add a sentence to personalize the principle to yourself. Journal your experiences as you proceed with this **GLORY** study guide.

_____

_____

_____

_____

_____

_____

_____

_____

_____

_____

_____

_____

_____

_____

_____

_____

G

L

O

R

Y

The Glory of Living
Study Guide

Chapter Seven

Squeezing the Glory Out

"God uses resistance…to 'squeeze' His glory out of us" (p. 116).

Can you recall a time when God's glory changed you permanently? If so, what happened? (see p. 114)

_____

_____

Rate your level of perseverance. Are you 1) very patient, 2) totally enduring, 3) edgy, but trying to trust, 4) filled with complaints? Which of these best describes you and why? (see p. 115)

_____

_____

If someone were to look inside you right now, what would they find that's good? What would they find that's in need of change? (see p. 116)

_____

_____

1

G
L
O
R
Y

Gain
Perspective

"Growth occurs only as we overcome resistance and obstacles."

G
L
O
R
Y

Gain
Perspective

continued

Think about a time when you were at the end of your resources and God stepped in (see p. 117). What happened?

_____

_____

Dr. Munroe outlines God's public relations campaign: "God's power, nature, character, and glory can be seen by the most people as He works through...difficulties" (p. 119). How does this work? Have you seen this divine marketing technique work? How?

_____

_____

_____

When God called Moses from the burning bush he revealed Himself (see Ex. 3:6-10). How has He revealed Himself to you? (see p. 120)

_____

_____

"There comes a time to stop resisting God..." (p. 125). Do you know when to quit resisting your Creator? Have your ever resisted Him to a point of disaster? What did you learn from this?

_____

_____

_____

Look at Matthew 5:48. How can Jesus ask us to be perfect, when we are imperfect by nature? (see p. 114)

_____

_____

Read Philippians 1:6. How confident are you of this verse? When things are most grim, are you confident? When things are going well, are you most confident? (see p. 114)

_____

_____

_____

_____

Based on First Peter 1:6-9, how has the refiner's fire produced "gold" in you? What is your "gold"? (see p. 115)

_____

_____

Look at Exodus 14:31. What does "feared the Lord" mean? How does someone "put their trust" in God? (see p. 127)

_____

_____

2

G
L
O
R
Y

Look
It Up

"Consider
it pure
joy...when
you face
trials of
many
kinds..."

3

G
L
O
R
Y

Order
Your
Thoughts

"If life has
you 'in a
squeeze,'
don't despair;
that's a good
place to be."

What are your current trials and tests? What glory do you believe will be exposed if you mature during these times? (see p. 116)

_____

_____

"One important key to understanding the Bible is to recognize that it is God-centered, not man-centered" (p. 118). What does this mean to your use of the Word in your life?

_____

_____

Recall a time when you stepped out in obedience, only to feel God perform a "squeeze play" on you (see p. 122). What was the result? Was the experience worth the result? Do you recognize "squeeze plays" as they are coming, or just after the fact?

_____

_____

_____

Have you ever felt circumstances tighten their grip around your finances? What is your normal response to such a time? What should it be? (see p. 123)

_____

_____

_____

"Circumstances are God's gifts to our glory" (p. 117). How can you use your current challenges as tools to witness to non-believing acquaintances?

_____

_____

Dr. Munroe reminds us that testimonies are usually based on how God has brought us through difficult times (see p. 118). What is your current testimony that could be shared with someone?

_____

_____

_____

_____

When God called from the burning bush, Moses had many objections as to why he shouldn't go to Egypt. "Moses, however, was afraid to manifest his glory" (p. 121). Are you afraid to manifest your glory? What are your excuses? Rehearse in your heart God's answer to each of your objections.

_____

_____

_____

_____

_____

4

G
L
O
R
Y

Rehearse
Your Plan
to Change

"We show the
world how
big God is by
the trials He
brings us
through."

G
L
O
R
Y

Rehearse
Your Plan
to Change

continued

When the people of Israel faced the Red Sea on one side and Pharaoh's army on the other (see Ex. 14:5-9), "Moses' response revealed his complete and utter trust in the Lord" (p. 126). What is the key to responding this way in the face of challenges? How can we respond, as Moses did, with complete and utter trust in the Lord?

_____

_____

_____

_____

5

G
L
O
R
Y

Your Next
Step to Glory

"As believers
we are 'jars of
clay' that
contain God's
glory, and
squeezing
us will bring
it out."

John 16:33 includes "take heart!" How do you do this? Take a moment to apply faith to each hard-pressing issue you face today (see p. 117). Find a promise in the Word for each situation and let it "live in you" so that you will "overcome the evil one" (see 1 Jn. 2:14b).

_____

_____

Identify an area where your will is in opposition to God's will. Cleanse your head from your distorted logic. Melt your heart from its stubbornness and give in to God (see p. 125).

_____

_____

_____

Is there something standing in the way of the Lord's delivering you? What does it take to stand firm and watch God work? Use the Word and worship to make your stand against that thing that is prohibiting your freedom (see p. 127).

_____

_____

_____

_____

_____

_____

Dr. Munroe asks us to change our viewpoint (see p. 128). Ask the Lord to take away your self-centered worldview and get a biblical God-centered worldview.

_____

_____

_____

_____

_____

_____

_____

G
L
O
R
Y

Your Next
Step to Glory

continued

G
L
O
R
Y

SUMMARY

Reread the ten principles on page 129. Highlight the words pressure, trials, problems, obstacles, and hardships. Name something after each principle that directly relates to it. You've just created a list of your answers! Journal your experiences as you proceed with this **GLORY** study guide.

_____

_____

_____

_____

_____

_____

_____

_____

_____

_____

_____

_____

_____

_____

_____

_____

Chapter Eight

Jesus—Revealing God's Glory

"Jesus gives us the perfect model of a truly successful life" (p. 132).

Dr. Munroe tells us that all of Jesus' life pointed toward "one defining moment," which was the cross (see p. 132). Do you think your life is pointing toward "one defining moment"? Are you aware of your specific purpose on earth?

_____

_____

"Through His obedience Jesus glorified both Himself and His Father" (p. 133). How does our obedience glorify both ourselves and our Father?

_____

_____

Jesus is the Life-Giver. Explain how Jesus gives you life (see p. 134).

_____

_____

1

G
L
O
R
Y

Gain
Perspective

"The
purpose
of life is
to reveal
our glory."

G
L
O
R
Y

Gain
Perspective

continued

Why is an extraordinary God interested in the ordinary affairs of men? (see p. 137)

_____

_____

Dr. Munroe tells us that Jesus glorified the Father through His work (see p. 143). You are God's worker. What line of work is it? How does your work express God's glory?

_____

_____

_____

God is the "Manufacturer" and you are the "product" (p. 144). Write God's advertising slogan for you, His product.

_____

_____

Explain the difference between unity and union. Why is union so important? (see p. 144)

_____

_____

_____

_____

Look at John 17:4. How was God's glory evidenced through Jesus? What work did He do? Do we have to do a similar work to enable a similar evidence of glory? (see p. 132)

_____

_____

_____

Read John 1:1-5. Jesus = God in the flesh (see p. 132). How does His example challenge you to shine brightly in your world?

_____

_____

Based on John 1:14,18, how are you able to live your life full of grace and truth? How do these show your glory? (see pp. 134-135)

_____

_____

_____

_____

Look at John 8:28-29. Jesus always did what pleased the Father. Define what is pleasing to the Father (see p. 139).

_____

_____

2

G
L
O
R
Y

Look
It Up

Jesus:
"I have given them the glory that You gave me."
John 17:22

3

G
L
O
R
Y

Order
Your
Thoughts

"Jesus was
the full
manifes-
tation of
God's
glory in
the flesh."

Dr. Munroe writes, "God is the core reality that underlies everything that exists..." (p. 135). How has humanism distorted this truth? How can you keep your mind from being distorted?

_____

_____

"Sometimes God allow things to 'run out' in order to reveal His glory" (p. 137). What have you "run out of" recently? Did God reveal His glory? Why or why not? What is necessary for you to let His glory be revealed the next time you "run out"?

_____

_____

_____

Dr. Munroe tells us that God "doesn't get much exposure during good times" (p. 141). Is this a difficult truth for you to accept? Why or why not?

_____

_____

"What is glory? True nature. Jesus gave us the same nature that He and the Father share" (p. 144). What is your true nature? How does the awareness of your true nature make you feel?

_____

_____

_____

We know that one day every knee will bow and every tongue will confess that Jesus is Lord (see Phil. 2:8-11). Does knowing this change the way you pray for each of your unbelieving co-workers or neighbors? They will believe some day. Pray it will be before they die (see p. 133).

_____

_____

Among your family members, how are you able to demonstrate God's grace? God's truth? God's unchanging glory? Plan a "grace demonstration" for one member of your family this week (see p. 136).

_____

_____

On page 140, Dr. Munroe paraphrases Jesus' summary of His life on earth. Write your name on the blanks below.

SUMMARY OF _____'S LIFE:

WHEN WE LOOK AT _____WE
        SEE GOD!

What is necessary for this to be a true statement?

_____

_____

_____

4

G
L
O
R
Y

Rehearse
Your Plan
to Change

"...character-
istic qualities
of His
nature...
best seen
through...
the lives of
believers"

G
L
O
R
Y

Rehearse
Your Plan
to Change

continue

Dr. Munroe writes, "Our work should reveal Jesus in us, who in turn reveals the Father, who is our Source" (p. 144). Think of ways you can reveal Jesus through your work. Plan for these throughout your week.

_____

_____

_____

_____

_____

5

G
L
O
R
Y

Your Next
Step to Glory

"When life
throws you
a curve,
remember
it's a
glory curve."

Take several minutes to let God hand you His grace (charis), favor, and gifts (see p. 135). What does He give to you today? How will you let your glory show with use of this favor or gift?

_____

_____

_____

_____

Praise in God's presence, no matter what situation you face. Take the time to praise; it's worth it! Let His glory flood you to bring out the very best in you today (see p. 138).

_____

_____

Meditate on John 8:42. You also have not come on your own. Rehearse the thought, "I have not come on my own; but God sends me." Take this throughout your day. Dwell on its wisdom for your life (see p. 139).

_____

_____

_____

_____

_____

Dr. Munroe states, "Glory comes out in our work, not our worship" (p. 144). Prepare yourself. Use your day's work to work out God's glory in you today.

_____

_____

_____

_____

_____

_____

_____

5

G
L
O
R
Y

Your Next Step to Glory

"When life throws you a curve, remember it's a glory curve."

G L O R Y

SUMMARY

Reread the 11 principles on page 145. Circle the word glory that you will find in ten of the principles. Summarize these with one overarching statement. Journal your experiences as you proceed with this **GLORY** study guide.

_____

_____

_____

_____

_____

_____

_____

_____

_____

_____

_____

_____

_____

_____

The Glory of Living
Study Guide

Chapter Nine

Releasing the Glory

"Your full glory is everything you were born to do that you haven't done yet..." (p. 148).

Dr. Munroe tells us that we must "get 'in sync' with our glory" (p. 149). How can a person do this? What is the process?

_____

_____

_____

_____

Do we ever have a "day off" from glorifying God? Why are we to "expose some stuff" each day we are alive? (see p. 152)

_____

_____

_____

_____

1

G
L
O
R
Y

Gain
Perspective

"...the key to godliness is a personal love relationship with God..."

G
L
O
R
Y

Gain
Perspective

continued

"To be godly means to be just like God. Is it possible for human beings to be like God?" (p. 153) Answer this question in your own words. Why is faith so important in this?

_____

_____

_____

_____

Dr. Munroe tells us that the best way to bring our glory out is to make demands on it (see p. 154). Think of your glory bank account. How does one make deposits into this bank so that there are no non-sufficient fund notices when a withdrawal is placed?

_____

_____

_____

_____

"Godliness comes at a personal cost..." (p. 154). What is the cost factor to obtain godliness?

_____

_____

_____

_____

Are you in touch with the "ultimate you"? Do you know the "true person hidden inside that no one has ever really seen"? How does one "go public" with their glory? How will you? (see pp. 154-455)

_____

_____

Why does our attempt to show God's glory frighten us? (see p. 158)

_____

_____

G
L
O
R
Y

Gain
Perspective

continued

Read John 12:23,27-28. List four attributes of God's nature that glorify Himself. Beside these list a work of your hands that demonstrates each attribute (see p. 149).

_____

_____

_____

_____

Look at First Timothy 4:7-8. What would a schedule for a "training camp" in godliness include? Does your schedule include these things? (see p. 153)

_____

_____

_____

2

G
L
O
R
Y

Look
It Up

"...that we
may live
peaceful
and quiet
lives in all
godliness
and holiness"
1 Tim. 2:2

**G
L
O
R
Y**

Look
It Up

continued

Read Second Peter 1:3-7. According to Dr. Munroe, what are your true needs for life and godliness? Why don't these seem to be enough? (see pp. 153-154)

_____

_____

_____

_____

_____

_____

Based on Matthew 5:14-16, how obvious are you? Is your light under a basket of fear? Is your city behind a mountain of other priorities? Purpose to put your light and city in their proper places (see pp. 156-157).

_____

_____

_____

_____

_____

_____

_____

_____

What would the waiting and watching world say about your life, if given the opportunity? Are there adjustments you desire to make? (see p. 151)

_____

_____

Dr. Munroe writes, "Another way we glorify God is by displaying His likeness" (p. 151). How will you uphold His reputation through displaying His likeness?

_____

_____

_____

_____

Dr. Munroe tells us that "A third way we glorify God is by displaying His character" (p. 151). Has anyone ever confused you with God? Why or why not? How can you become more of a reminder to others of your Father?

_____

_____

_____

_____

_____

3

G
L
O
R
Y

Order
Your
Thoughts

"We do not glorify God by our religious activities, but by displaying His nature, character, and attitude."

G
L
O
R
Y

Order
Your
Thoughts

continued

"We also glorify God by showing creation the attitude of God" (p. 152). Take an attitude check. Does your attitude reflect God? Use a one word description of your attitude for each of the following:

FAMILY _____

JOB _____

MINISTRY _____

OTHER SIGNIFICANT RELATIONSHIPS _____

_____

_____

4

G
L
O
R
Y

Rehearse
Your Plan
to Change

"Where
glory is
concerned,
don't expect
an easy road."

Dr. Munroe tells us that each of us has a "moment of glory" (see p. 150). What steps must you take to pursue your "moment of glory"?

_____

_____

On a scale of one to ten, rate yourself on the things we are to "show off" from Galatians 5:22b-23a. What can you do in the next three months to have the ratings rise by one point in at least three categories? (see p. 151)

Love _____	Joy _____	Peace _____
Patience _____	Kindness _____	Goodness _____
Faithfulness _____	Gentleness _____	Self Control _____

_____

_____

Read First Timothy 6:11. From what are we to flee? What are we to pursue? What is your strategy for fleeing what you should and pursuing what you ought? (see p. 153)

G
L
O
R
Y

Rehearse
Your Plan
to Change

continued

_____

_____

_____

_____

_____

_____

_____

_____

Have you ever done a spiritual gifts assessment? You could make use of tools that are readily available to do so, or have your leaders or peers give you an inventory of what they see in you (see pp. 148-149).

_____

_____

_____

_____

5

G
L
O
R
Y

Your Next
Step to Glory

"There
must be a
moment in
life...when
we and
our glory
become
'one.' "

Take some time to glorify God's name. Let Him reveal His glory to you. Journal what He speaks in your heart. Make your prayer, "Father, bring out of me all of Your expectations in order to protect Your reputation" (see p. 150).

_____

_____

Where have you been guilty of hiding behind the statement "I'm only human"? (see p. 154). Repent for this. Ask God to help your life become a revelation of the nature and likeness of God.

_____

_____

Dr. Munroe says, "The purpose of life is to get rid of our glory. Living is all about glory manifestation" (p. 155). Focus your mind on your purpose in life. Apply God's grace to it as you bask in His presence. Determine in your heart that you will rid yourself of all your glory before you die.

_____

_____

Read the first full paragraph on page 158. Meditate on its truths and let God speak to your heart as your pray.

_____

_____

SUMMARY

Reread the ten principles on page 160. After each principle, write a sentence of confirmation, personalizing the principle in your life. Journal your experiences as you proceed with this **GLORY** study guide.

_____

_____

_____

_____

_____

_____

_____

_____

_____

_____

_____

_____

_____

_____

G
L
O
R
Y

255 ❖

The Glory of Living
Study Guide

Chapter Ten

The Fragrance of Glory

"Our glory exists not for our own benefit but for others" (p. 162).

Dr. Munroe asks if you have thought that you have had more problems since you became a believer than before. Is this true for you? Does the explanation at the top of page 164 seem to fit your experience?

_____

_____

"Satisfaction Guaranteed!" God wants to place this stamp of approval on us. How does God test us, His product, so that His warranty will be valid? (see p. 166)

_____

_____

"Growth is glory exposed...Maturity is...the full exercise of potential" (p. 169). Can people measure your growth? Do others see your maturity?

_____

_____

1

G
L
O
R
Y

Gain
Perspective

"God will do whatever He needs to do to get His glory out of us."

G
L
O
R
Y

Gain
Perspective

continued

"As long as we follow our own initiative, God doesn't have to act" (p. 170). How can you keep your initiative active?

_____

_____

ASSIGNMENT: EARTH. How might you describe yourself according to the following standards: (see p. 172)

BOLD _____

POWERFUL _____

DILIGENT _____

PASSIONATE _____

You are God's "SWAT" team for all unbelievers. What does that mean to you? (see p. 174)

_____

_____

_____

_____

Why do we need to welcome risks and challenges? (see p. 174)

_____

_____

Look at Second Corinthians 2:14-16. Are there acquaintances or family members who do NOT like the smell of your glory? Do others like it? (see p. 164)

_____

_____

_____

Read Isaiah 48:10-11. In your own words, explain why God tests us (see p. 166).

_____

_____

Read the Beatitudes in Matthew 5:3-10. From this passage, chart out the list of those who are blessed and their distinct blessings. Are these natural traits or do you have to work at them? (see p. 171)

Poor in spirit = kingdom of heaven   Mourn = _____

_____

_____

Look at Romans 8:17-21. What does "the creation waits in eager expectation" mean to you? (see p. 173)

_____

_____

2

G
L
O
R
Y

Look
It Up

"For the earth will be filled with the knowledge of the glory of the Lord..."
Hab. 2:14

3

G
L
O
R
Y

Order
Your
Thoughts

"Crushing
really is
the key to
releasing
the glory
of God."

If you were to describe the fragrance of your glory, what would you say? Why? (see p. 162)

_____

_____

_____

What does God want to reveal in you? What needs to be stripped from you before it can be revealed? (see p. 162)

_____

_____

_____

On page 165, Dr. Munroe outlines three secrets for manifesting the glory of God. How do these three secrets apply to your life?

_____

_____

_____

Like Shadrach, Meshach, and Abednego, are you willing to be afflicted in order for God to be glorified? It may not be as drastic as a furnace; it might come as subtly as a misunderstanding (see p. 169).

_____

_____

"Have you ever thought of yourself as 'the aroma of Christ' or the 'fragrance of life'?" (p. 164) If you see yourself this way, it should change the way you approach your circumstances. How?

_____

_____

What demands are being placed on your potential right now? How should you focus your attention? How will challenge bring out God's glory? How will pressure bring forth His purpose? (see p. 166)

_____

_____

_____

_____

Fill in the newspaper headline below. After you have filled it in decide how you will release the glory given to you (see p. 173).

HEADLINE: Large God With Infinite Universe

Gives Little _____

(your name)

the Purpose and Vision to _____

(your call)

Name some people who need your glory right now. Plan to expose them to it in the next week (see p. 173).

_____

_____

4

G
L
O
R
Y

Rehearse
Your Plan
to Change

"No matter
how 'bad'
our day
may seem,
it is a
good day
for the glory."

5

G
L
O
R
Y

Your Next
Step to Glory

"God alone is
the 'guilty'
party. He
alone is
responsible
for creation."

"Our problem is that so many of us are all bottled up and sealed tight in jobs or circumstances or attitudes that restrict us" (p. 163). Confess these to God. Repent from restricting your fragrance. Let God prepare you for the release of your scent.

_____

_____

"Thank God for what you've been going through...for the glory He is bringing out of you...for the privilege of exposing His glory....for the revelation He has given you...for the confidence and assurance He has given you that you can handle everything that you're going through...for the promise that He will not place on you more than you can bear" (pp. 164-165). So thank Him!

_____

_____

Dr. Munroe tells us that we often appreciate the growth we see in ourselves following a challenging situation (see p. 169). Praise God right now for the things He has brought you through and the specific way in which you grew.

_____

_____

"We should never ask God, 'Why me?'" (p. 170) Open yourself up to God right now so that He might use you. This means you will expect Him to give you incentives to grow. Tell Him you will receive these with joy.

_____

_____

SUMMARY

Reread the ten principles on page 175. Insert your name into each of these principles at the appropriate place. If you truly believe these, you will pray them into your life. Journal your experiences as you proceed with this **GLORY** study guide.

_____

_____

_____

_____

_____

_____

_____

_____

_____

_____

_____

_____

G

L

O

R

Y

Bahamas

Faith Ministries International

The Diplomat Center
Carmichael Road
P.O. Box N-9583
Nassau, Bahamas

TEL: (242) 341-6444
FAX: (242) 361-2260

**Website:
http://www.bfmmm.com**

IN PURSUIT OF PURPOSE

Best-selling author Myles Munroe reveals here the key to personal fulfillment: purpose. We must pursue purpose because our fulfillment in life depends upon our becoming what we were born to be and do. *In Pursuit of Purpose* will guide you on that path to finding purpose.

ISBN 1-56043-103-2

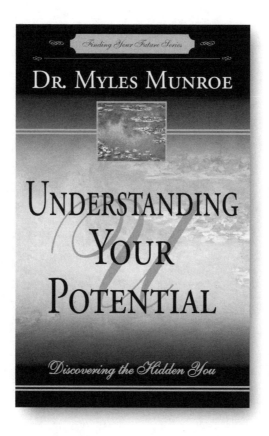

UNDERSTANDING YOUR POTENTIAL

This is a motivating, provocative look at the awesome potential trapped within you, waiting to be realized. This book will cause you to be uncomfortable with your present state of accomplishment and dissatisfied with resting on your past success.

ISBN 1-56043-046-X

RELEASING YOUR POTENTIAL

Here is a complete, integrated, principles-centered approach to releasing the awesome potential trapped within you. If you are frustrated by your dreams, ideas, and visions, this book will show you a step-by-step pathway to releasing your potential and igniting the wheels of purpose and productivity.

ISBN 1-56043-072-9

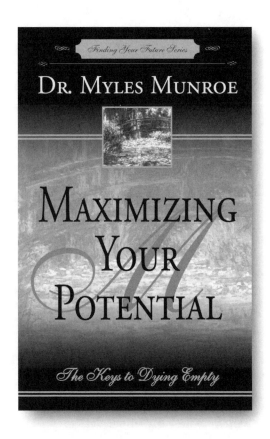

MAXIMIZING YOUR POTENTIAL

Are you bored with your latest success? Maybe you're frustrated at the prospect of retirement. This book will refire your passion for living! Learn to maximize the God-given potential lying dormant inside you through the practical, integrated, and penetrating concepts shared in this book. Go for the max—die empty!

ISBN 1-56043-105-9

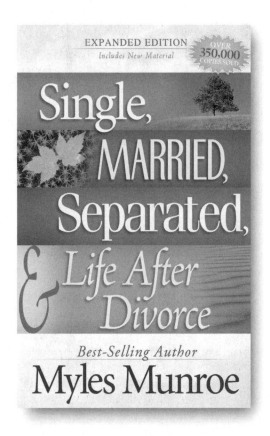

SINGLE, MARRIED, SEPARATED, & LIFE AFTER DIVORCE

Myles Munroe, deals with the complicated and emotion-laden issues of relationships, lack of loving relationships and the severance of relationships in this powerful little book. Looking at the volatile issue of divorce and its aftermath, Dr. Munroe shares the counsel he has given to thousands of people.

ISBN 0-7684-2202-7

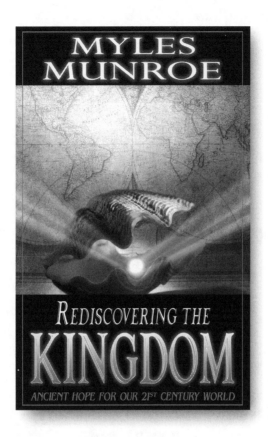

REDISCOVERING THE KINDGOM

As Dr. Munroe unveils the reality and power of the Kingdom you will be challenged to the core of your religious soul as you are exposed to realities that few are declaring in these days. *Rediscovering the Kingdom* will defy almost every concept you have about *religion*, as he shifts the focus away from religion toward *the* ultimate issue—the Kingdom of God.

Hardback ISBN 0-7684-2217-5
Paperback ISBN 0-7684-2257-4

Additional copies of this book and other
book titles from DESTINY IMAGE are
available at your local bookstore.

For a bookstore near you, call 1-800-722-6774.

Send a request for a catalog to:

Destiny Image® Publishers, Inc.

P.O. Box 310
Shippensburg, PA 17257-0310

*"Speaking to the Purposes of God for This
Generation and for the Generations to Come"*

For a complete list of our titles,
visit us at www.destinyimage.com